BORDER-LAKI TERRIER

A Breed Guide

SEAN FRAIN

Email: holrob@hotmail.co.uk

*Please note that some photos are very old
& are thus not of the best quality

BULL GHYLL PUBLICATIONS

CONTENTS

Introduction

1. SHAPING TYPE

2. UNFASHIONABLE

3. CHOOSING A PUPPY & A NAME

4. REARING, FEEDING & TRAINING

5. STARTING THE YOUNGSTER

6. SHOWS

7. TERRIERS AT WORK

8. TO BREED OR NOT TO BREED?

9. FIRST AID & CARE OF THE ELDERLY TERRIER

10. LIST OF TERRIER NAMES

Introduction
[Pages 4-8]

The Border-Lakeland terrier is a truly ancient breed and terriers of similar type were once common throughout the country. They were originally created for ridding farms and smallholdings of rats, foxes, badgers, polecats and other predatory beasts, but nowadays the Border-Lakeland is popular as a pet, show dog, and as a working terrier still, though Patterdale terriers seem to have risen massively in popularity in recent years and Border-Lakeland terriers have thus lost some ground to these as both a worker and as a family pet.

David Brian Plummer described such terriers as the original stock which gave rise to both Border and Lakeland terriers. I must state that I agree with him, though that is not the full story, as we shall see. Several old photographs depict Border-Lakeland type terriers and they are very similar to today's breed, with often poor shaggy coats being a predominant feature. Much has been written about poor coat not being desirable on terriers required to work in the high places of Northern England, but the truth is that seemingly unsuitable jackets were produced on many of the early terriers. Several of the modern Border-Lakeland terriers continue to produce poor coats, yet they seem to thrive, even as working dogs, in spite of the severity of the weather.

Conditions in Lakeland and surrounding areas can be severe, and that is undoubtedly an understatement. There is a recorded account of a 1963 Shepherds Meet at the Queen's Head, Troutbeck, which illustrates the point. Such meets by that time were not quite the grand affairs they once were, but they were still very important social occasions for farmers and villagers who lived remote lives.

Modern transportation means gathering lost sheep is far easier these days, but at one time such meets were held so that stray sheep could be reunited with their particular shepherd and flock. This meet was once held at the Kirkstone Pass Inn; one of the highest public houses in the

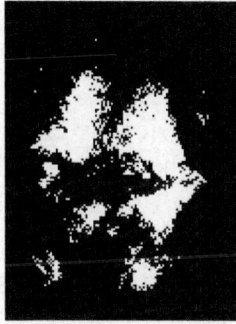

1
SHAPING TYPE
[Pages 9-26]

Work, above all else, is what has shaped Border-Lakeland terriers (also known as fell terriers) and the northern terrain of England has possibly exercised the most influence in this regard. The Lake District, as is well documented, is where many of such strains began and the harsh landscape of this area has undoubtedly had a huge influence on the early bloodlines, but such terriers, or at least terriers of very similar type, were also common in the Borders of Scotland, Northumberland, County Durham, North Yorkshire, Lancashire, and Wales.

Much of the terrain of Wales is mountainous, so it is surely only logical to conclude that Welsh breeders played an important part in producing working terriers hardy enough to cope with often hostile conditions. Such terriers were also found in the low country of Wales, where rich farmland and woodland was the hunting grounds of these little tykes, as well as rivers and streams when otter was the summer quarry, but, nevertheless, they would still need to be hardy little souls in order to cope with the demands of pest control in an area where predator numbers were high.

These Welsh-bred terriers were often known by the names of the areas in which they were produced, or worked, in much the same way as early Lake District terriers were named, until they became known by the all-encompassing name of Welsh terrier by the latter-half of the nineteenth century.

Lake District Terrier Names

Lake District working terriers were known by all kinds of names, with the scruffy, shaggy type (the ancestor of modern Border-Lakeland terriers) often just being referred to as a coloured working terrier, as though it wasn't worthy of a proper name. During the nineteenth century a hard-coated, leggy terrier with a powerful head began breeding true to type and these became known as Patterdale terriers, as such types were undoubtedly once used with the Patterdale Hounds (where they may have originated).

This name quickly became fashionable and any terrier of similar type was given the name of Patterdale, no matter which district it came from (such terriers were different from the Patterdale terrier of today). Dan Pattinson of the Patterdale Foxhounds was an influential breeder of working terriers and it may have been his stock that was first given the name of Patterdale terrier, though this can only be educated guesswork.

The Influence of Northern Fox Earths

The predominant type of earth foxes use in Cumbria, once separated into three counties; Cumberland, Westmorland and Lancashire, are rocky dens in crags, borrans, or rockpiles left by man below old quarries. Such rock has been discarded by the quarrymen over several hundreds of years and the piles just get higher and higher after every quarry clear-out. Such rockpiles are favourite haunts for foxes, especially those which are being hotly pursued by a pack of fell foxhounds, yet they have proven to be great death-traps to working terriers sent in after a fox.

Some terriers have succeeded in working foxes out of such piles of 'rubbish' (rocks unsuitable for shaping into slate, or stones for the building trade), while others have never been seen again. Such 'rubbish' piles are not suited to digging, as they are usually so unstable that digging is impossible, so a terrier sent into such a place has to do its best to get out under its own steam, so to speak, or end its days there.

country, which has long associations with both the Coniston and Ullswater Foxhounds. It was moved to the Queen's Head at Troutbeck and there the farmers gathered on that grim autumn day in 1963. Previous to the meet being held at the high inn at Kirkstone, where hounds were 'lowsed' (loosed) onto Red Screes opposite the inn, this Shepherds Meet had been held on the High Street range on the eastern side of the Troutbeck Valley, over two thousand feet above sea level.

The Kirkstone Pass Inn where traditional Shepherds Meets were once held (late 19th century)

A grey sheet of rain swept up the Troutbeck Valley that morning and the farmers stared into their beers around the bar and tables of the Queen's Head, the fierce flames of a roaring coal fire reflected in the cool depths of their ale. Many shook their heads in wonder, as the seemingly impenetrable wall of persistently heavy rain obliterated everything, making it almost impossible to discern where earth met sky. Everything was grey and dull, dank and dark, drear in the extreme. The farmers simply couldn't believe that Anthony Chapman, Huntsman of the Coniston Foxhounds, had 'lowsed' his 'hoonds' in the morning.

Chapman's terriers also went along with him, of that one can be certain, which demonstrated just how tough and hardy these small tykes have to be. That was a day that demonstrated just why many fell pack huntsmen favoured a tight, hard jacket on a terrier, despite the fact that many ran-on several with poor coats over the years.

John Bulman of Langdale, Master and Huntsman of the Windermere Harriers and a real Lakeland character who was also a much-respected farmer, arrived later that morning, but left hounds in the van, as he deemed it unsafe to hunt the lower vale of Troutbeck, lest hounds frighten sheep into the swollen becks (at least this gave him a good excuse to remain dry!). Anthony Chapman and the hardier followers arrived back at the inn later that day, the grey sheet of incessant rain still falling, sodden to the bone, but cheerful and happy. Then a 'good auld' tattie-pot supper and a sing-song were enjoyed into the late evening, or perhaps even into the early hours. This was a traditional way of finishing off a Shepherds Meet.

The northern districts seem to have been the stronghold of the ancestors of today's strains, but very similar types, though perhaps with better coats, were found in Wales. There is also written evidence which suggests that black and tan terriers similar to Border-Lakelands were used with hunts in the south-east of England as early as the eighteenth century. There is also an old newspaper account of a black and tan terrier of similar type being sold to a farmer just north of Manchester, by a chap from Skipton in North Yorkshire. This was during the nineteenth century and the account goes on to demonstrate not only the intelligence of such terriers, but also their sheer hardiness.

The terrier arrived at the train station near Manchester and was left in the Porter's Office for the farmer to collect. The farmer was from Harwood Fields, which was also the site of weavers' cottages and a small mill, as well as quite a large farm. Somehow the little terrier managed to get out of the box it had been transported in and it simply disappeared. The farmer later learned that the terrier, after a lengthy journey of thirteen days, had finally arrived back at its former home in Skipton; rather dirty, bedraggled and a little thinner, but in fine condition generally. Reading between the lines, it seems the farmer then got his money back and the terrier remained at its former home. Only the hardest-hearted person could have gone through with such a sale after that incredible journey and obvious devotion.

Harry Lancaster with the Coniston Foxhounds & terriers on frozen Windermere in the severe winter of 1895; terriers need to be tough to work in such conditions

The Border and Lakeland terrier both originated from stock similar in type to the Border-Lakeland of today, yet the old strains, despite not producing world-beating show dogs, have survived and that has surely to be put down to the sheer versatility and character-full nature of these plucky and incredibly friendly little tykes. Most people very quickly fall in-love with Border-Lakeland terriers and anyone who has owned one, or who has been in the company of this breed of terrier for more than a few minutes, will understand why. Border-Lakeland terriers have a wide appeal, as they are grand little working dogs, make great family pets which generally love children, and provide hours of entertainment to those who enjoy their cheerful nature and often-comical antics.

They make grand little show dogs too, though there is generally no prize money, or glory in showing this breed. Just a good day out at a country show and maybe a rosette or two, or, if you are very fortunate, maybe the odd trophy or two! In short, Border-Lakeland terriers are great fun to own, are generally easy enough to train and are usually quiet around the house. In fact, with some of them being so quiet in nature it is often the case that you hardly know they are around.

Tommy Dobson with hounds; note the Border-Lakeland type in the foreground (late 19th century)

Unfortunately, many a terrier has ended its days in one of these quarryman's rockpiles.

Terriers at the Coniston Foxhounds during the 1950s – shaped by the landscape of the Lakeland fells

Borrans, or bields (the Lakeland name 'bield' means 'shelter' and so any earth used by a fox in Cumbria can be called a 'bield,' though this name is generally used when describing borrans), are also very popular sanctuaries for foxes, hunted or otherwise, and some of them are huge. If you have ever seen the video, Todhunter and the Fox, or have hunted with a pack of fell foxhounds yourself, you will be familiar with the size of some of these rock dens. Similar piles of rock are found in parts of Lancashire and Derbyshire, yet few can be compared to the Lake District borrans.

John Finney has hunted a few small hounds on the moorlands and fells of the north for several years and he runs on a few terriers which he has used mostly for fox control in some bad earths, yet he admits that he has rarely had to deal with the kind of earths the fell pack huntsmen and terriermen have had to contend with over the years. John knows of several rocky earths used by foxes and one of these, similar in every way to a Lakeland borran, yet nowhere near as vast, is a bad place to work.

Hounds have several times marked the place eagerly, but when he has loosed a terrier, it has been unable to get far enough into the borran to reach its fox. The terrier has almost been screaming with excitement because of the smell of its nearby quarry, but simply cannot get in far enough to put any pressure on. Foxes, he says, usually don't bolt when they know they are safe in such frequently used strongholds.

It is the rock of the Lake District and other parts of the country, particularly the northern regions, which has shaped type in what we know today as the Border-Lakeland terrier, yet they have proven useful in every type of earth, from dug-out rabbit holes to the worst of the borrans of Lakeland, or the cairns of Scotland for that matter. And so the first and foremost standard for modern Border-Lakelands is that they must be workmanlike and full of spirit, or 'fire,' as the Lakeland terrier enthusiast would put it.

Temperament

This does not mean that they should be aggressive. In fact, aggression towards other dogs, or people come to that, is most undesirable. Border-Lakelands should be of a quiet nature, as they were once frequently kennelled with hounds, or several other terriers, and thus needed to get on well with

absolutely freezing – classed as arctic conditions by meteorologists, in fact. The injuries and the shock of the ice-cold conditions saw-off the poor terrier in only a few minutes.

The old Patterdale type with the Eskdale & Ennerdale Foxhounds at the end of the 19th century – note the harsh jacket

A second terrier had been put in and this proved very game, as it eventually killed the fox, but not before having its jaw broken. The Huntsman, Dan Pattinson, then carried his terrier home, where he treated its injuries and fed and bedded down his hounds. The terrier was up and about a few days later, then it went on to make a full recovery, minus a few teeth, including two fangs, which had been pulled out by the fox. It may have been during Dan Pattinson's stint at the Patterdale Foxhounds that Border-Lakeland type terriers began to be named 'Patterdales.'

Shows had begun to take off in a big way during the 1860s and rivalry meant many were given names to reflect the areas in which they were bred, or worked. The terriers working in the Ullswater district were described as 'shaggy-coated' in 1878, which suggests the coat-type was not of the really tight and harsh variety. It seems that few terriers had such hard and wiry coats in those days.

John Finney doesn't put too much emphasis on coat, as he has had some with very poor jackets, while others have been hard-coated. One he mentions, a hard-coated terrier called Fettler, never suffered in any way from the elements, no matter how bad the weather, no matter at what time of year he was out. On the other hand though, he also tells of another terrier, Turk, which had one of the poorest jackets he has ever seen on a terrier, yet he too never suffered when the weather turned nasty. John has been out in all kinds of conditions, from freezing temperatures well into the minus figures, to severe snow blizzards which made him resemble a snowman in less than a minute, yet has rarely seen his terriers badly affected. His hounds, he stresses, have smooth coats nowhere near as dense as those of his terriers, yet they seem to cope well, so why should his terriers suffer badly?

The only terrier of his which sometimes showed signs of suffering from the elements was his bitch Myrt, which was a slape-coated (a Lakeland term for a dense, smooth coat, with perhaps a slight wiriness to it) Patterdale/Border-Lakeland cross. When strong winds blew and icy rain fell, then he has seen her trying to get out of it and trembling with cold whenever she was stood around "doing nowt." But he has never had a terrier go off its feet through cold affliction, so has never worried too much about the type of jacket found on the terriers he has worked for several years. Another terrier bitch he had, Briar, a lightly worked old fashioned Border-Lakeland type, had a very poor coat too, yet she seemed to cope with any weather condition without too many problems. Terriermen will never agree when it comes to the kind of jacket they favour.

Terriers have been used at otter for hundreds of years in Cumberland and at one spot an otter was seen going into a drain. The terriers were fetched and the owner was an experienced Lake District breeder who worked his terriers regularly. He entered one of his breed, which took a little time getting to its otter, but eventually succeeded and bolted it out into the icy water, as this occurred on December 1st 1890.

The author of the report (whom I suspect was Rawdon Lee who wrote a popular book about Fox terriers) then went on to describe the kind of terriers he bred. Their colour was red, tan, blue grizzle and black and tan. They were around twenty pounds in weight, with some lighter and others a little heavier. They had straight legs with plenty of length to them, and were long in the back. They had shaggy coats and quite big ears. He referred to these as "crossbreds." He had started his strain from stock belonging to the Honourable H. M. Beresford and the first of such stock he saw at work was later killed by a badger, during a dig organised by the writer of the otter-hunting report. It seems he had the terrier on loan from Beresford and was using it to breed stock, and for work too.

Another otter-hunting report was from July 11th 1846 and a terrier named Chancellor was put into a pool at Gillhead, near Birkett Houses. The otter dragged the terrier under and it came up spluttering and bleeding. Mr Cloudsdale of the Crown Hotel, Bowness, and Robert Dacre of Lythe, both keen hunters, were in attendance, though it isn't clear who owned the terrier. Surely a decent coat was required when docked however as this could result in the wound failing to heal and thus your dog would have to be put to sleep in the end. I know that the chances of this happening are very slim, but surely it isn't worth risking.

The Importance of Spanning

A chest that is capable of being spanned is the usual standard for Border-Lakeland terriers, which, after all, are a working breed. This is not a Lake District, or even a northern tradition, but one that originated centuries ago when small dogs began to be bred for use underground. Spanning a terrier is carried out by placing one's hands directly behind the shoulders. If the tips of the thumbs meet, together with the tips of the fingers, then a terrier is said to be easily spannable. If the tips of the thumbs and the tips of the middle fingers only, meet, then a terrier remains spannable, but has a chest that is on the bigger size. If a person with medium sized hands cannot span a terrier, then its chest is too large generally. That terrier would then struggle to get to a fox in smaller earths.

This rule is not as important to those who only keep a terrier as a pet, but as a worker and a show dog, being able to span is essential. True, not all who keep Border-Lakelands and other working breeds of terrier use them to earth, preferring to use them at rabbit and rat. Even so, whilst drawing for rabbits in particular, it is likely that such a worker would at some time or other encounter a fox earth and enter. Terriers with large chests, those that are not capable of being spanned, are far more likely to get themselves stuck inside an earth, than those that are capable of being spanned. So it is an important aspect to consider.

A subject that goes well with spanning is to make certain that, if a terrier will be worked underground, it is not overweight when doing so. True, when enjoying the summer rest period some terriers will put a little weight on, as they are not nearly as active as they are during hunting time, but that weight should be walked off by the time work begins once more. Just as a terrier with too large a chest will run the risk of becoming trapped underground, so will a terrier carrying too much weight.

Good Bone, Head & Jaw Strength

I have heard that some breeders of working terriers, in order to attempt to stop their puppy from growing too big to work average fox earths, have fed them as lightly as possible. I know that this sounds ridiculous and that it is hard to believe that such idiots actually exist, but I am assured that this is not an urban myth, though I wish it was.

The Blencathra Foxhounds at the Lodore Hotel in the 1930s –note the good head on the terrier to the right

Never deny proper feeding to a growing puppy, no matter what advice you may be given to the contrary. The size a dog will reach is determined by its genes, not by what goes into its food bowl, or, rather, by what does not go into its food bowl. Such a practice will only produce a weakling of an animal with poor bone structure, weak teeth and weak jaw; in other words, a sickly animal lacking proper vitamins and other essential goodness. Put plainly – neglect and cruelty. A puppy should put on plenty of flesh, so that as an adult it has sound bone structure, good muscle, sound teeth and a strong jaw. Such qualities are vital. A dog can have rather a narrow muzzle, yet can still have a strong jaw.

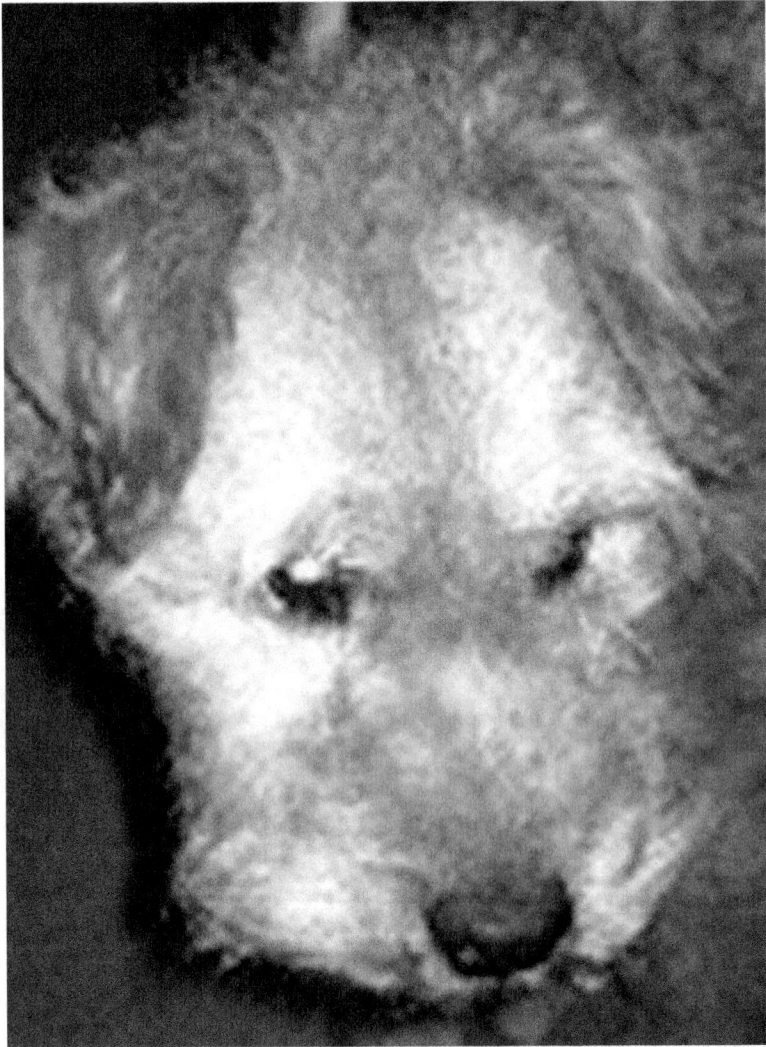

My terrier, Beck – a good strong head

The teeth should meet in a scissor-bite, with the bottom row of front teeth just slightly behind the top row. The bottom fangs should just slip comfortably into place in front of the top fangs. This gives the jaw maximum strength. Undershot mouths are a fault found on strains that have been too closely inbred and such a fault is not desirable. If you wish to show your terrier, then an undershot mouth will be a great disadvantage.

John Finney tells a couple of tales that illustrate just how essential it is for puppies to develop fully. One day several years ago he was drawing through a spinney with his pack, with his terrier, Fettler, loose so that he could more easily slip into the stickpiles and thickset gorse and bramble bushes around the wood. Finney drew a blank, but quickly noticed that Fettler was missing. There was only one earth in this spinney, just on the edge, which they had tried before drawing, so Fettler hadn't got in there. So he decided to have a look in a nearby tract of ancient oak and beech woodland, where he knew of an earth or two. Sure enough, he located his terrier who was steadily yapping in an earth that led under an old and very large tree.

The quarry was obviously going nowhere, so John decided to dig. He dug down close to the tree, but soon came upon massive tree roots which were never going to yield to his efforts to get past them. However, there was just enough room to dig a clearing and Fettler was now in sight and within easy reach. The terrier was hard at his foe, which held a handy position in among the roots. Fettler was not too hard a dog, though he could usually finish a fox that would not bolt. But it was obvious to John that his terrier was having a bit of a rough time here, so he now fetched Turk, who had been tied to a nearby fence post, and allowed him access at the spot he had opened up.

Turk was still a youngster at this time, being a son of Fettler, which in turn had been bred at one of the fell packs and had seen some service with hounds there, but he had matured and really settled to his work by the time of this dig. Fettler was a mix of Patterdale and Lakeland bloodlines, being descended from both Hardisty's Turk and Wilkinson's Rock. Turk's dam was Myrt, which bitch was a mix of Buck/Breay Patterdale blood, and Graham Ward unregistered Lakeland terrier blood. She was game and very hard. Myrt once bolted a dog fox, which came out of the earth in a sort of shocked and dazed state, after Myrt had attacked him with gusto. She then turned her attention to a vixen lodging in the same den and quickly finished it, though Finney didn't dig her out until the next morning, having been forced to leave the trapped bitch to ground after darkness forced him off the hill.

Turk somehow managed to get in ahead of Fettler, grabbing his quarry and, being such a strong dog, actually drawing it out gradually, despite the fact that it had the tree roots to use as an anchor. John was then very surprised to see that the foe Turk was drawing was actually a badger and not the fox he thought it was. A poor, weakly terrier not fed properly through the puppy and early adult stages would not have been capable of drawing a fox, let alone a badger (it is now illegal to dig badgers in the British Isles, though John did not set out to dig badgers and never did. Every badger he ever dug was accidental, his intentions always having been to dig out foxes. Badgers do use fox earths, so it is not always possible to avoid them), out of such a stronghold.

On another occasion, during a gloriously sunny day towards the back-end of the season, John's pack harried a couple of foxes around some dense gorse and Turk was with them. The foxes went to earth for some reason, into a rabbit hole they had enlarged, then John heard Turk baying. He fought his way through the extremely prickly herbage and located the earth, then prepared to dig. A large fox shot out of a hole a few feet to his right, but easily escaped. His hounds were not really capable of catching foxes on the run, so to speak, as John used them mostly for flushing, as well as for hunting scent, though mainly for short distances, till the fox went to ground. If a fox didn't go to ground within a reasonable distance, then hounds would usually lose it, though they have enjoyed some long hunts too, during those rare days when scent has been exceptionally 'holding.'

A few minutes later he noticed that Turk was getting a little nearer and so he cleared a space at the entrance. And there was Turk's rear-end, slowly coming towards him. Turk eventually drew a vixen from that earth and it took great strength for him to do so, as the narrow tunnel sides are used by foxes as an anchor under such circumstances. Again, only a fully developed terrier could be capable of such feats. Full development only comes by proper means – good feeding and regular exercise – so there can be no shortcuts in these essential matters.

The Lakeland landscape has to some degree shaped the bone, head and jaw strength of Border-Lakeland terriers, as they were originally bred to kill foxes below ground. This required great strength, as biting through to the windpipe in order to get a stranglehold on a fox takes a great deal of strength. Some terriers have been known to break the jaws of foxes in order to kill them, but this is not a desirable trait, as the terrier involved also usually receives some pretty horrific injuries, as with the Patterdale Foxhounds' terrier which died on Helvellyn after a bad mauling from a game fox. Of course, keeping terriers as pets puts much less emphasis on these qualities required for work, but any terrier possessing such qualities will be happy and healthy.

A Summary of Desirable Qualities

Size does vary, but it can be said that any Border-Lakeland terrier above fifteen inches is rather too big. Any below twelve inches are possibly a little too small. A tight, harsh coat is preferable, but several, possibly the majority, have shaggy jackets. Slape-coats are also found on some.

A terrier of this breed should be leggy and such legs are generally required to be straight, or as straight as possible. A terrier's movement must be free and easy, giving that impression of agility. They should have good bone, head and jaw strength, though head size varies considerably. A Border-Lakeland should also be capable of being spanned.

They should generally be of a quiet nature, but should also be full of life and character. Border-Lakelands should be workmanlike generally, but they should not be aggressive with people and other dogs. Most love children. They are generally tough little dogs, which should be capable of standing up well to an average winter. If a Border-Lakeland terrier doesn't enjoy going out on exercise, then there is something seriously wrong, as they love the outdoors, and no wonder, when you consider their active, even hectic, background.

The Ullswater Foxhounds were called out on April 12th 1890 in order to hunt down a fox which had taken some geese from Ed Thompson's farm. Hounds were 'lowsed' at Horn How Plantation and a fox was immediately away, with Chanter leading the pack as they hunted its line. 'Jacky' took them over St Sunday Crag, where foxy was hollered by David and Willie Wilson. He then took hounds over Glenmara Park and past Ed Thompson's farm, where he had earlier committed his crimes.

Reynard now went on past Deepdale Hall, up Gravel Moss and to earth at Harrison Crag, with Anthony Pool quickly getting to the place and entering his terrier, which was a "game un." The terrier found and yapped loudly at its fox, which Anthony Pool, after some hard work, managed to dig out. He then 'lowsed' 'Jacky' once again and it now dropped lower in. After a hunt in the vale, the fox was eventually caught in Mr Leck's field. It had been a fast and exciting hunt, which had resulted in the death of a marauding goose killer.

2
UNFASHIONABLE
[Pages 27-35]

The dog showing craze quickly took off after the first dog show was staged in 1859 in Newcastle. By the early 1860s classes for dog shows were being put on at agricultural shows countrywide and these quickly reached the Lake District where they took off in a big way. Classes for working terriers put on at Lakeland agricultural shows had several dozen entries, sometimes in each class, they became that popular, and by the beginning of the 1920s it was impossible to win with typical old fashioned fell, or Border-Lakeland, terriers, which then were known mostly as coloured working terriers, or simply as shaggy-coated working terriers.

The Influence of Shows
The Lakeland and Border terrier had emerged from the old fashioned type by this time and they became more popular as show dogs, though many continued to keep the old type working terriers, especially around the farms and the hunt kennels, though it is also true that the more showy Lakeland terrier began to be used at the fell packs, where they acquitted themselves well as workers. It is popularly stated that the Melbreak Hunt led the way in using the improved Lakeland terrier, but that is not entirely true, as each fell pack also had either a Huntsman, Whipper-in, or followers who worked the typey Lakeland with hounds. The

Blencathra and Ullswater packs, for instance, had several enthusiasts of the new type hunting with them, even before these terriers were given their new name at Keswick in 1912.

John Finney tells an interesting tale of attempting to do well at working terrier shows with the old fashioned type during the early 1980s when he showed his bitch, Rush, on a number of occasions. Rush was a superb worker and a superlative finder, as well as a bitch that could shift a fox that stood its ground. Finney used her in old mineshafts where an average working terrier could not hope to succeed. On several occasions she worked foxes out of such places successfully and without coming to any harm, living a full life until she was put to sleep at seventeen years of age due to rapidly failing health.

Rush was of general good type and she had a good harsh jacket too, but still, she did not have the sharp lines of the Lakeland terrier, nor the tidy looks of the Border terrier, so she performed poorly in the show ring, despite his entering her in the crossbred class. He made a point that a number of terrier lads put their unregistered Lakelands in the crossbred class in order to ensure winning a rosette and getting through to the championship at the end of the show. This made it impossible for the more old fashioned Border-Lakeland type to do well at shows and this may still be the case today. The sharp lines of the unregistered Lakeland terrier have become very fashionable during the past thirty years or so and so it is difficult to win with any other type these days. Yet some of these old fashioned types are excellent workers.

One of these was Zeb, owned by Charlie Swainson and sometimes worked alongside Finney and his pack. Zeb was bred out of stock from the Pennine Foxhounds at the beginning of the 1980s and he soon grew into both a handsome dog, and a grand little worker who could finish any fox which would not bolt. Finney remembers this dog well, stating that his sire did some excellent work at the Pennine and that his dam did some good work for another northern pack, a mounted one which hunted on the edge of the Pennine Chain.

One day Finney was out on the moors and right on the edge of Bilcombe Fell was a line of crags where foxes sometimes laid up. This was early autumn and sure enough a fox was marked in and Swainson entered his terrier, Zeb, which, Finney states, had a very strong and well muscled head. Zeb entered the rock den eagerly and then began pushing onto the fox. He finally reached it and settled down, only three or four feet from the surface, close to the top of the fell, behind the crags.

The old type soon became unfashionable

'Jacky' had got himself into a really tight space and probably couldn't have bolted if he had wanted to, so Zeb bayed strongly, then closed with his fox, while Charlie and his helpers dug down, shifting rocks out of the way as they made good progress. They finally broke through after an hour or more and Zeb had finished a healthy fox, but one that was obviously of that year's new crop from the spring.

Finney says that Charlie tried his hand at a bit of showing and that he did enjoy some success with Zeb, for he was very typey, as well as a worker, but that even he could not stand many of the farmers and fell pack followers continued to breed with working qualities alone in mind, with some decrying the pedigree Lakeland as a non-worker. This was a ridiculous claim, as many of the fell pack followers and huntsmen used Lakeland terriers, pedigree and unregistered stock improved using carefully selected bloodlines, at fox and otter in particular, though many were also used for badger digging.

Badgers & the Old Fashioned Type

The low country around Cockermouth, which stretches to the West Coast of Cumbria, was very often the testing grounds of Lakeland terriers pitted against badgers, as they were more readily found in these areas. Many of these pedigree and unregistered Lakeland terriers were badly mauled by badger, as they would not "give an inch" as the saying goes, and so several breeders preferred to use the old fashioned type, which was noted for having more sense at badger, when digging such fearsome quarry.

Badgers were not as common in those days as they are now, with badger sets found all over Lakeland these days, including on many of the fells where once they were rarely seen, but now and then the fell packs did come across one or two. This was the case when the Ullswater were invited to hunt the country around Sedbergh, which is now the Lunesdale Foxhounds hunting grounds.

Monday December 8th 1890 saw Joe Bowman cast his hounds for Cautley Crag, with Whipper-in Harry Watson assisting him. Hounds drew a blank at Cautley Crag, Hobdale Crag and Cold Bottom Scar, but a little way on began to speak to a bit of warm drag and it was reported that Bowman's ringing cry of "hark to him, hark," sent them all on in fine style, with a few hounds marking to ground shortly after. A terrier was put in and soon after, all were surprised to see a badger bolting out from among the rocks. Leader, the fell foxhound, lunged at it, but took a few bites for his troubles. The badger made for Cautley Holme, but the pack were on it, a little baffled at first because of never before having seen a badger, and they killed it, but not before it had left its mark on nearly every hound. It proved to be a sow badger of sixteen pounds in weight, which seems a little on the light side, so it was either only a few months of age, or there were lean pickings in the Cautley area for badgers. This area is close to where the Lunesdale Foxhounds are now kennelled.

An old fashioned type which gave rise to both Border & Lakeland terriers used with northern hunts

The hunters returned to the old inn at Cautley Head for refreshments and it was remarked upon that a badger had never been seen, or heard of, in that area before. Nutty Brown Ale was enjoyed by the party as they chatted and sung over the day's events.

A terrier must be both game and sensible to work such a hard fighting and strong boned creature such as a badger and the old fashioned strains of what are known these days as fell, or Border-Lakeland terriers, usually had these two qualities in abundance. True, some were badly mauled by foxes to the point of serious injury, which sometimes resulted in them dying, but generally speaking they worked their quarry well. Foxes can cause damage to even sensible terriers when in a commanding place, from which they can strike repeatedly, while the terrier is attempting to find a way of getting the best of its opponent.

Unfashionable, but a Survivor

Many of these sensible strains continued to be bred by farmers, villagers and fell pack followers in general, some from other parts of the country such as Wales and Manchester (old newspaper reports indicate that the Ullswater Foxhounds in particular had a lot of visitors from Manchester during the nineteenth century, and into the twentieth century, while all of the fell packs had close connections with Welsh packs and their followers, as well as some of the South-west England packs too).

It is such breeders that ensured the old strains would survive, despite being unfashionable with many. Border-Lakeland terriers of today, however, while still not having the sharp lines of the pedigree and unregistered Lakeland terrier, are not simply relics left over from the old days. Careful breeding has gone into the strains down through the decades of the twentieth century and into the new millennium. Some have used more typey Lakeland terriers in order to improve both coat and type, so that more success could be enjoyed at shows, while others have added outcrosses of Border terrier blood, in order to keep good adult dog for that matter. There are times when the nose can be dry and warm, but this is normal, as long as the nose returns to being cold and wet and the puppy or adult dog does not show any signs of sickliness.

Making a Choice

It is true to say that puppies differ in temperament and personality; some can be bold, approaching you and playing happily, while others may be a little reluctant. If a puppy is reluctant to approach you or your children, do not write it off; if this one appeals to you and your children in other ways. However, if the puppy is a trembling nervous wreck, then it is best to leave that one well alone. Choose the puppy that appeals to you, or, better still, allow your children to do the choosing. If possible though, go to view a litter without the children first of all. This can more easily be done if a litter is local and if the breeder will allow you a second viewing with your children, which any decent breeder would be happy to do.

This allows you to avoid possible broken hearts among your children. If they love one of the puppies, but it is obviously sickly, or the whole litter is not suitable, then you will have to walk away and this could mean great disappointment to kiddies. If a litter is not local, then your wife/husband or a friend could go along and supervise the kiddies in the car, while you have a quick look over the litter. If suitable, the children can then be asked in. This method could save much heartache.

Children and dogs often share some sort of mysterious affinity and a puppy chosen by children and reared with children often grows into a very well-adjusted and agreeable animal with plenty of personality. Border-Lakeland terriers already have plenty of personality, but one brought up in a family environment seems to develop that extra-special something that cannot be explained. If you take your children along to view a litter, and you must, then allow them to handle the litter and play with them. Keep an eye on them, of course, making certain they are gentle with the youngsters, but by doing this you will have plenty of time to bone structure and that all-important sensibleness. So, no, Border-Lakeland terriers these days are not simply descended from the old type that gave rise to both Border and Lakeland terriers, but are often the result of several outcrosses back to those Lakeland and Border terriers they originally produced. The Patterdale terrier too, is closely related to modern Border-Lakeland terriers, as well as the unregistered Lakeland terrier. This means that temperament and type differs among modern stock, but still there are some very good bloodlines around today, some of which are worked, others of which are not worked. But generally speaking, most make great family pets and grand little workers, if the would-be owner is so inclined.

Border-Lakeland (old fashioned fell type), Lakeland, Border & Patterdale terriers are all closely related

observe the litter closely.

If you cannot carry out a first viewing alone, do not allow children to go straight to the puppies and make a choice, as you must first make certain all are healthy and free of skin problems or any other obvious complaints. Once you have decided a litter is suitable then you should encourage your children to make their choice. If a breeder will not allow you sufficient time for this, then do not rush in and purchase a puppy. Make it clear that you need to look them over carefully *before* making a choice.

Have a look in the ears and make sure they are clean. Allow for a little wax here and there, but if the ears are full of wax and black bits everywhere, it is likely they have either canker, or ear mites, or possibly both. Puppies that look thinly fleshed, with large pot bellies, are sure to be full of worms. Dirty ears and pot bellies usually accompany one another. This is a neglectful breeder who should not be dealt with. The dam will also be full of worms and will have been throughout pregnancy and rearing, so keep well clear of these sickly puppies, which will likely grow into sickly adults. You will likely never be away from the vets if you purchase such a puppy, which will probably cost you the equivalent of a second mortgage! A good breeder will have wormed the puppies at least a couple of days before beginning to sell his litter.

Purchasing, Transportation & the New Home

If all is well health-wise and one of the puppies appeals to you and your family, then seal the deal. A good sturdy cardboard box with newspaper in the bottom will be ideal for transporting the puppy home. It is best not to allow your children, or anyone else for that matter, to hold the puppy while on the move, as an accident, or having to brake sharply, could kill or injure the youngster. It will be much safer in a sturdy box placed on the floor in front of the passenger seat.

Before leaving the seller's home ask if you can take a small amount of the bedding from the whelping box with you, which will have all of the scents of the dam and litter on it, thus comforting the puppy for a day or two until it gets more familiar with its new home. It is also good to ask for a small amount of food, so that you can mix it with the food you will be using, which method cuts down considerably on stomach upsets. This is not essential, as a puppy will soon get settled with a new diet, but a steady change of feed is always the best option.

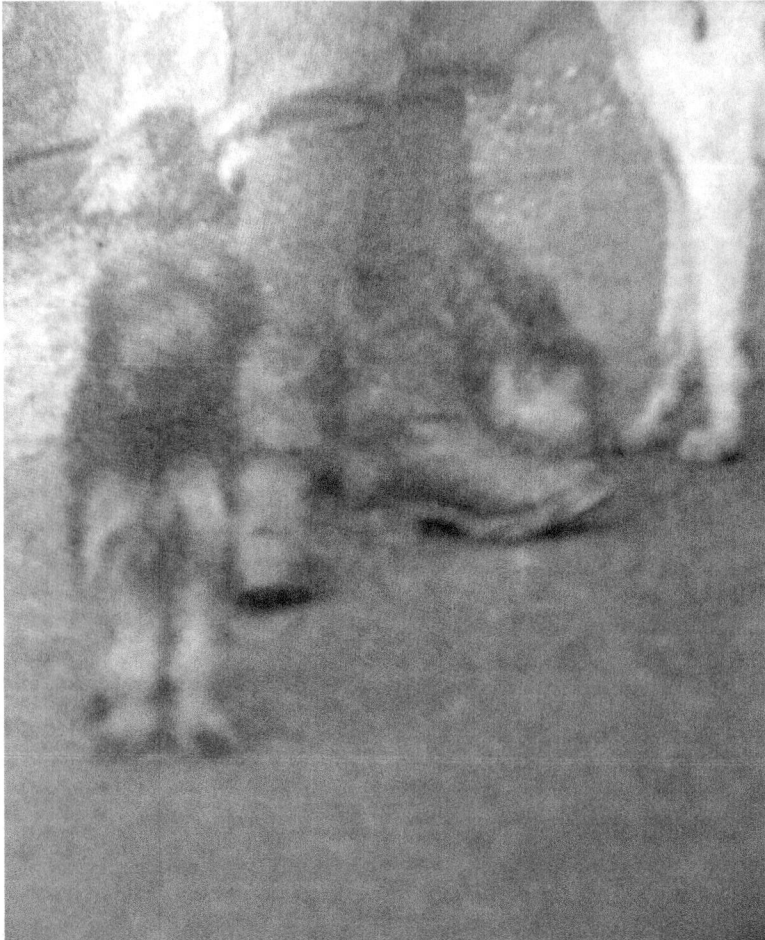

Workers of the early 20th century

The Future Worker
If you are choosing a puppy with work in mind, then it is

always the wisest option to purchase stock from working bloodlines. There are plenty of reputable breeders of working Border-Lakeland type terriers and these can quite easily be found through the pages of publications such as the *Countryman's Weekly*. When working terriers it is always best to be familiar with the laws of the land of the country in which you live and to work your terriers within these laws.

If coat type is an issue, then it is best to ask to see both parents, if at all possible, so that you can check on the jackets. If both have good coats, then likely the puppies will have too, though there are no guarantees. John Finney has bred a few litters over the years and he put his hard-coated dog, Fettler, onto a bitch with a harsh, close type of jacket. One pup came slape-coated and another came with a very poor open coat, with the rest having extremely good jackets. And when a puppy is just eight weeks of age it can be difficult knowing what coat type will finally turn out like. It can be a bit of a gamble, but the best chance of getting a puppy with a good coat is to buy one whose parents have tight, harsh jackets.

The eventual size of a terrier, an important matter when it comes to working stock, is also difficult to ascertain, but if both parents are of a decent size for work and are of a size to be spanned properly, then it is likely that their offspring will not be too big either. If a puppy has massive paws, then it will undoubtedly grow to be of a larger size, but small paws on a puppy will indicate that it will not usually grow too big. A terrier that grows too big for many earths, however, can still be very useful for bushing work.

Settling in the New Puppy

Puppies differ in temperament and some settle in almost immediately, while others take a day or two to respond to their new environment. If your puppy is a bit sulky, then by all means nurse it on your lap until it becomes a little bolder and more comfortable, but if it is boisterous and untroubled by the journey and new surroundings, then by all means play with the puppy. However a puppy responds to its new home and owners, it will only take a day or two to become more settled, quickly finding its place in the family arrangement.

Choosing a Suitable Name

The first thing to do after purchasing a new puppy is to give it a name, as becoming familiar with its name is essential to socialising and training. It can be a good thing to allow children to name their new pet, but be prepared for a name that you would usually never even consider. A friend of mine had a chocolate coloured Border/Lakeland and he asked his children to name her, which they did. 'Biscuit' was how she became known and that, surely, was always going to be the obvious choice.

Many Border/Lakeland terriers have unusual names and John Finney always gives his terriers unconventional ones. Rush, Fettler, Breck, Turk, Scrag (scrag-end was a cheap cut of meat that was once popular among the working classes of the north) Tarn and Gryke are just a few of the names he has used for his working Border/Lakeland terriers and there are a whole host of other names, mostly originating in the Lakes, that are given to this breed (see the list of names in chapter ten for ideas).

Whatever name you or your children choose, make certain it trips off the tongue comfortably and suits your terrier, as it will be stuck with it for the next decade and more. It is important to get the naming of terriers right, as it is not a good idea to change a name once the puppy has got familiar with it and is responding to its name; this would only cause confusion and confusion makes a dog unsettled and thus unhappy. Dogs need familiarity to be content and thus settled, so choose a suitable name and stick to it.

4
REARING, FEEDING & TRAINING
[Pages 43-54]

Allow the puppy to settle in for a day or two and then take it to the vets for its first injection, which should be administered at eight weeks of age. The last puppy I had injected was given its inoculations at eight and twelve weeks of age, which is different to the previous methods used on puppies in the past. Methods may vary, but your vet will advise you of correct dates on which to receive the second injection. Also, get your puppy micro-chipped as soon as possible according to your vet's advice. This is vital just in case you do lose your dog at some point, so that it can easily be found and reunited with its owner. Losing a dog is very distressing, yet it is so easily done. You just lose concentration for only a minute or two and your dog can have seemingly disappeared into thin-air, so it is always the best policy to micro-chip. It will become law in some countries to micro-chip in the near future, but it is because you care about your dog that you take such precautionary measures, not because the law tells you to do so.

The Importance of Early Socialising
Vets have come to realise the importance of socialising puppies as early as possible. Dogs which turn aggressive to other dogs or even people have usually not been properly socialised when puppies, so vets advise that, a few days after the first injection, once some immunity has built up, you

take your puppy to friends and relatives houses where there are children and dogs. Better still, invite sensible friends and family round who have well behaved children and dogs and allow the puppy to play out in the garden, but not out on the street.

You must still be cautious and careful until after that second injection. Getting your puppy familiar with children and other dogs during those four weeks that a puppy isn't allowed out into public areas will do much to develop a good future temperament. Make certain, however, that such socialising sessions are always supervised by an adult. Children must not be rough with a young puppy, as this could cause later aggression. Older dogs need to be checked if they get a little too rough with a puppy too. An atmosphere of playfulness and happiness must be the norm for a puppy, as this will allow it to grow into a well adjusted adult dog, though discipline is also important when necessary.

A couple of days after the second and final injection exercise can begin, but remember not to take the youngster on lengthy walks during those early days. Its paws must harden first of all, as they may become a little tender to begin with, especially after walking along paths and roads. The wide open spaces and encounters with other people and dogs will be intimidating at first, so short, but regular, walks are best at this time. Remember, wild dogs, as puppies in particular, can fall prey to predators such as eagles, or big cats, so it is a natural instinct to avoid open spaces where they are more vulnerable. That is why many puppies seem afraid to go on walks to begin with, but experience will teach them that they are perfectly safe and then they will soon come to relish exercise periods.

Those early walks are an important part of the socialising process and it is important to allow your puppy, while secured on a lead, to meet with other friendly dogs. You may wish to join a puppy group in order to make the most of socialising opportunities, but the same results can be obtained by taking your puppy to parks and other public places where there are friendly dogs, as well as into town where they will become familiar with crowds of people. The importance of such socialising cannot be stressed enough. It is vital that puppies get out among other dogs and people, particularly children, as soon as possible. Lead training is vital early on too, but we will deal with this subject a little later.

Feeding & Watering

Fresh water should always be available to puppies and adult dogs alike, and water bowls should be cleaned regularly, as a build up of germs can easily result in stomach upsets. Stomach upsets can kill puppies, so cleanliness with regard to both water bowls and food bowls is essential. The hard work as regards feeding has been done for the dog owner these days, by manufacturers of complete dog foods which I have found to be excellent and very convenient when you live a busy life.

There are several good brands of complete dog food on the market, but do not conclude that the cheaper end are no good. I have used a cheap supermarket brand for a number of years now and it is both very affordable and very good, as my dogs thrive on it. There is less waste when using complete dry foods and my dogs eat grass and vomit far less than they did when I fed them brawn, or tinned meat, with a mixer. Their health is superb and that is borne-out by their eagerness to enjoy long walks and their oily, glossy coats.

Use a specially formulated puppy feed until your terrier reaches the age of four to six months, as this will more easily be swallowed and digested. The first meal of the day should be one of cereal, softened with warm, not hot, milk. I give weetabix, or an equivalent, for the first meal of the day and the amount should be just one at eight weeks of age. The puppy food can be given at lunch time, then again in the evening. Just before bed, give a light feed of half a weetabix, which will help the puppy to settle for the night. If you are working through the day and cannot provide a lunchtime feed, then put in two weetabix for the morning feed. A bowl of fresh water should be available at all times, but when a young puppy, do not use a large bowl that is full, as a puppy could fall in and drown. Use a small bowl with not too much water in, till the puppy has grown and such an accident will not occur. Remember to regularly check the amount of water in a bowl, as dogs, especially after being fed, will drink often. Make sure such things as mop buckets are not left around full of water. An inquisitive puppy can so easily fall in and drown.

Avoiding Obesity

Once a puppy has reached the age of three months cut out one of the meals, dropping to three a day. This can be dropped to just two meals at the age of four months, then one meal from the age of eight months. Of course, you may wish to continue feeding twice a day, but make certain that you do not provide too much food. Most dogs are greedy and will eat until they burst, so regulate their weight. An obese dog is an unhealthy dog. Likewise, an emaciated dog is an unhealthy and neglected dog, so always keep an eye on their weight. A dog should look just right, which may seem a daft statement to make, but you will soon come to know the weight at which your dog is at its best. It should be well muscled and covered in enough flesh to avoid the bones protruding, but layers of fat should be avoided. Diabetes and heart disease will constantly threaten a fat dog, so if you notice your terrier putting too much weight on, then simply cut down on the amount of food you provide. This is also important when working your terrier.

Feeding the Worker

A fat working terrier will put much strain on its heart, but there is also another danger to consider. When going to earth a fat terrier can more easily become trapped below ground, as it tries to push through narrow places where it would normally be able to get if it wasn't fat. So a good working weight is one of leanness (though not skinniness) and muscle. If your Border-Lakeland is one of the rough-haired variety, then use your hand to check on the weight, as the fur can hide the facts.

Just feel the back-end and if the pin bones are protruding and the flesh is really sunken at the ribs, then increase the food until a more suitable weight is reached. The pin bones should just be felt on the hand when pressing on the back-end. There should be flesh around them, but they shouldn't be well covered. This is only a general guide to weight and you will quickly learn to regulate weight yourself, without advice from anyone. If the ribs, pin bones and spine are protruding on any dog, then it is in a neglected and emaciated condition and needs to be fed much more. I am sure most owners would never let an animal get into such a state and so keeping a close eye on weight, when a dog is both a puppy and an adult, is vital. Also, if an animal is fat, getting out of breath quickly and spending much of its time panting after any kind of exertion, then it is in an obese condition and having your dog fat is killing it with kindness, so learn to find a good balance with a feeding regime, remembering that a healthy dog is a happy dog.

House Training

This form of training is simple, but often the lesson takes time to be learned. Whenever your puppy urinates or defecates in the home, show it the offending mess and say 'no' in a firm voice, then carry it out into the garden while saying 'outside.' This must be repeated at every opportunity. Never allow a puppy to mess without punishment. This lesson can be repeated in a morning when you rise, as there will likely be a mess waiting for you. Whenever your puppy 'goes' outdoors. Give plenty of praise, especially if it goes to the door asking to be let out. If, however, your terrier continues to make a mess during the night, it may be best to use a training cage. These are also excellent if a youngster is inclined to chew furniture when left alone. All-metal cages are best, as they last much longer than those with plastic trays. The confined space will usually prevent a puppy from making a mess in its own bed.

Basic Training – Come, Sit, Lie-down, Stay

The first thing to do is to get your terrier to come when called. I use a simple, but very effective method. First get your puppy familiar with its name and use it in such a way that the youngster associates pleasure with that name, so use it often when playing, praising and stroking. Use its name when putting its food bowl down and, when it is out in the garden, call it in while shaking its favourite bag of treats. Milk drops for dogs are ideal for this, as they are both cheap and irresistible to a puppy. When your puppy comes to you, praise it and give it one of the treats.

Training a Border-Lakeland to 'sit'

Do this every time it responds when called and in no time at all it will associate responding to your summons with a tasty morsel. This can be carried on into adulthood, or stopped when your dog has grown older and is readily obedient. It is entirely up to you if you will, or will not, keep up the giving of treats when commands are obeyed. My own dogs grow out of needing a treat in order to be obedient and thus I rarely use them after puppyhood.

Training to sit is simple. Simply call the puppy to you and press down on its back-end while commanding in a firm, but not loud, or angry, voice for it to 'sit.' A similar method is used when commanding your puppy to lie-down. Put it into the sitting position first and tell it to 'lie-down,' while gently pulling out the front legs so that it has little choice but to obey. When responding to any command make certain you give plenty of praise and affection.

The stay command is a little more difficult to teach, but a puppy will soon learn. Get your youngster to either sit or lie-down and then command it to 'stay,' while putting your hand in front of its face. Repeat this firm command and only give praise if your puppy does not move. Remember to give praise while it remains in the stay position, not after it has moved, as this will only serve to confuse the trainee, for it will think the reward, or praise, is for moving rather than staying. Repeat these lessons as regularly as possible, but do not overdo things. Keep training sessions brief and enjoyable, playing little games after each session in order to instil pleasurable associations into your puppy.

This is vital. If a puppy grows bored and gradually develops a loathing for training sessions, then you will have done more damage than good, so brief and enjoyable must be your goal when engaging in basic training. Sit, lie-down and stay are simple enough lessons to teach and instil and these are usually enough for anyone who work their terriers, or who keep them as pets or show dogs. More advanced training is something I have never engaged in, so I would not even attempt to try to tell others how to carry out such training. Basic training has proved to be enough in my household and

I pride myself on having well behaved dogs which are well socialised from being puppies.

Training to 'lie-down' & 'stay'

Lead Training & Heel

Sit, lie-down and stay can be taught in the home and garden from as early as eight weeks of age, as can lead training. It is good to have completed lead training basics by the time the puppy has finished its inoculations and it can now be exercised in any suitable place. Lead training is very simple. Put on the puppy collar and attach the lead, allowing the puppy to drag it around for a short while, but not allowing it to chew the lead. Then pick the lead up and gently pull at it. You will likely have to drag your puppy for a while, but very gently, until it begins to walk in the direction in which it is led. Keep this up regularly, but again keep the sessions short and pleasurable. Begin in the home, then carry on out in the garden and once inoculations are completed the lead training can continue at exercise proper. The lesson will quickly be learned and your trainee will soon come to love its walks.

 Dragging a puppy gently is usually the way to get it to walk with you, but then a puppy can begin pulling and this is most annoying, yet is easily corrected early on. Simply jerk the lead, pulling the puppy back sharply, while firmly commanding it to 'heel.' This training technique must be implemented early in lead training and you must be both persistent and consistent in heel training. The youngster will catch on in the end, though some take longer than others. I have never had a failure using normal leads and collars, so have never gone in for such things as choker chains to aid heel training, so I feel I cannot recommend them. If you are firm and do not tolerate any messing around, your puppy will soon come to realise this and it will obey you in the end, though be patient, as some do take longer than others to catch on.

Another good training tip is to hold training sessions in different locations, so that the youngster becomes familiar with being obedient to your commands in all kinds of places and situations. It is good to train at home and in the garden, which are the most convenient places in this busy world, but public parks, out in the countryside, even in towns and cities, are other locations where training sessions can be held. Your puppy must become familiar with traffic, crowds of people, cats, other dogs, and, for those of us who enjoy walks in the countryside, farm livestock. There is nothing worse than to have one's pet dog chasing sheep or cattle. Not only is this very embarrassing, but it can be harmful to the victim, as well as your pet, as a farmer will likely shoot a dog that chases his stock. Sheep are very sensitive creatures and they can so easily die after being badly stressed. In-lamb ewes can abort after being chased by a dog, even if only for a minute or two. The milk of cows can be spoiled if the animal is badly stressed, so it is important to teach a dog early in its life that it must leave farm livestock well alone.

Breaking to Livestock

It isn't difficult to break a young dog to livestock, though if you purchase an adult that isn't trained in this regard, then it may be impossible to stop it from chasing sheep, cattle, or fowl such as chickens. In this instance it is best to keep the dog on a lead when in places where livestock will be encountered, though such an animal cannot usually be trusted anywhere as it will likely not only chase cats (cats can be encountered almost anywhere, in town or country alike), but will attack and kill them too.

This is yet another good reason for purchasing a puppy, especially if you are inexperienced when it comes to livestock breaking. It is child's play to break to farm animals with puppies. Simply secure your young dog on a lead and walk it among livestock. You could ask the farmer's permission to go into his fields with the animals, or simply train from the side of a country lane or footpath where the animals are plainly in view. Be careful, however, with cattle. It is best to train from the side of a country lane when it comes to large animals such as cows, as these can herd together and charge.

Cattle act according to instinct, protecting their calves from the dog which they see as a threat, but the person with the dog can be trampled to death in such situations, while the dog easily runs away to safety. So if walking in the field, stick to the edges so that you can easily get through or under the fence and thus remain safe. In the minds of cattle, dogs can be a real threat to calves. In America, for instance, coyotes will prey on calves and they have even been known to attack adult cattle if hungry enough. Coyotes are simply wild dogs, so the instinct of cattle to see off dogs which come too near is only natural. Even if there are no calves in a field, still do not go in unless you and your dog can exit very quickly and safely.

If you ever do get into a position where you find yourself in the middle of a field with a herd of large cattle coming at you, then loose the dog and get out of their way. They will simply chase the dog as they are not interested in humans. Your dog will easily get away. Just concentrate on your own safety without panicking. Before carrying out livestock training it is best to have your youngster coming to you on command and obeying simple and basic instructions such as the sit, lie-down and stay commands.

When walking near livestock with your trainee secured on a suitably strong lead, jerk the lead back and command your puppy to 'leave' in a firm voice which leaves no room for disobedience. Be diligent in keeping such training regular and consistent, but again make certain the sessions are short, with praise and fun games aplenty at the end of each session. This method should be employed with all kinds of livestock, including cats you come across on the street, sheep, cattle, horses, chickens, ducks, geese, or even more exotic animals you may encounter on farms these days such as lamas. Some youngsters will learn almost immediately, while others take time and gradually lose interest in chasing other animals they come across at exercise. For these, more stringent methods can be used in order to instil the lesson more quickly and more firmly.

Carry a thin leather lead in your other hand and as soon as your pet shows any interest in livestock of any kind, crack the lead on the ground in front of it. This acts to distract the thoughts and works well. Use the firm 'leave' command while doing this, together with a strong jerk of the lead attached to the trainee, and the lesson is instilled yet further. Again, regular and consistent sessions are essential. You must be firm in training to leave livestock alone, transmitting to the young trainee that you will not tolerate such behaviour. It may take time, but your pet will eventually learn the lesson and then you can enjoy relaxed walks in the countryside in the full knowledge that your dog will not chase sheep, cattle, horses etc. Such training is vital, but what if, after all your efforts, the youngster weakens and chases livestock?

The first thing to do is not to panic, but to become that figure of authority who has been carrying out training for the past few weeks or months. A firm command of 'leave' repeated several times may stop the offender in its tracks, but if not try the 'stay' command, as this alternative can work. Whilst doing this get yourself into a position, if possible, where you can get between the dog and the sheep, or whatever animal it is chasing, and then crack the lead on the ground several times in front of the dog while firmly commanding it to 'leave.' This should work. Once you have your dog safely secured on a lead, show it in no uncertain terms that it is in your bad books for at least the next few minutes. Never give praise or any kind of treat after such an offence, as it will believe it is being rewarded for its efforts. Livestock training should then continue for a time, until you feel your dog has learnt its lesson. Even if your trainee seems well and truly trustworthy with livestock, provide a refresher course at least once a year throughout its lifetime, just to make certain. Trained dogs can occasionally weaken if the lesson isn't repeated, but reminders will avoid any future problems.

Livestock breaking is essential for all owners of game terriers, but most of all it is essential for those who work their terriers in the countryside and mostly on farmland where livestock grazes. Having your terrier chase livestock is the surest way of losing permission to hunt over land and the terrier itself might also be shot and thus lost forever. It is important that those who work terriers are diligent in this regard, as farmers will simply not tolerate the irresponsible on their land. It does take effort to train a dog to leave livestock alone, but the peace of mind one can enjoy while in the countryside makes that effort more than worthwhile.

5
STARTING THE YOUNGSTER
[Pages 55-66]

Many and varied have been the methods of entering Border-Lakeland terriers to more traditional quarry such as the fox and the older hunting folk of the fells employed methods which best suited them. When the more-fiery Lakeland terrier began to breed true to type during the latter part of the nineteenth century it was found that these matured very quickly and most were literally begging for work by the age of nine months, and so several breeders did begin working their charges to large quarry at such a young age, though many Border-Lakeland terriers that gave rise to both Lakeland and Border terriers which were later recognized by the Kennel Club, would not have been ready for work at just nine months. Several of this breed, perhaps most in fact, took time to mature and so some breeders didn't start them at fox, badger and otter until they were at least twelve months of age, though several terriers were not started until fifteen or even eighteen months of age.

Two Reasons for Not Entering too Early
This was for two reasons; firstly, because the terriers were not mentally mature enough to cope with a hard-fighting fox, or worse still an incredibly tough badger or fast-striking otter. Early encounters ruined terriers not ready for such large quarry, putting many off earth work for life or making them too hard, which often resulted in them lacking the

sense to stay out of trouble and avoid bad maulings, the resultant wounds sometimes being fatal. And, secondly, the bones and teeth are not fully developed until the age of eighteen months and so the more discerning breeders held young terriers back until both fully developed and mentally mature. This ensured that such young entries would take to their work very naturally and that they would be able to cope both mentally and physically with the rough-and-tumble life Border-Lakeland terriers lived when working rough country.

George Henry Long of Egremont was one who favoured Lakeland terriers and he felt that any Lakeland was ready for earth work at fox by the age of nine months. His father, a Lake District character called Peter Long, entered his stock at such an age and so he passed this method onto his son. Willie Irving was another who began using some of his terriers at fox by the age of nine months and he learned much of his trade from Willie Porter at the Eskdale and Ennerdale Foxhounds, so these methods were passed on to the next generation. Many, though, as already stated, held their charges back until they reached full maturity at eighteen months and this was undoubtedly the most sensible method.

Some also hunted rats and rabbits and entering to such quarry was usually started at around five or six months. Rabbits would be the first quarry and then rats, the terriers being a little older when entering to rats, which could bite hard and put youngsters off. George Henry Long entered to rat at just six months, but most held them back until around eight months or so. Polecats and pinemartens were also hunted until the mid-1900s and terriers would not be entered to these until seven months at least, probably a little later. These creatures, known in Lakeland as 'foumarts' and 'sweetmarts' respectively, struck fast and bit hard, hanging on with jaws like steel traps, so terriers were generally a little on the older side when first starting at such quarry.

'Sandy's' Entering Methods

There is an interesting account regarding the entering of a terrier worked by Willie Sanderson of Carlisle. Willie

'Sandy' Sanderson was a Carlisle butcher who was incredibly keen on hunting otters through the spring and summer months. He whipped-in to Billy Robinson, who was a renowned Huntsman of the Carlisle Otterhounds and who eventually relinquished his position to the young 'Sandy' (who went on to become an even more celebrated Huntsman).

An Egremont terrier which worked with otterhounds

'Sandy' had many terriers while hunting the Carlisle Otterhounds, which were originally kennelled at Catholic Street in the city. The Carlisle Otterhounds, which became the Carlisle and District Otterhounds, were formed from a pack kennelled at Carlisle and the Maryport Otterhounds, which were owned by a Mr Irving of Maryport.

'Sandy' took over as Huntsman in 1864 and their first meet as the new Carlisle Otterhounds was held on Tuesday April 26th 1864. Sanderson owned a terrier called Billy at the time and he described how he had entered the terrier a few years before. Billy was actually a bull terrier, but not the typical Staffordshire or English type. He was a small bull terrier common in the North of England during the eighteenth and nineteenth centuries and he only weighed twenty-two pounds, which made him a handy size for use below ground. Miners used these tiny bull terriers for fox and badger digging, as well as for ratting and dog fighting.

Billy was kept off small quarry like rats and rabbits and was entered straight to polecats (foumarts) at just seven months of age. Willie stated that his terrier just played with his first polecat, but the second bit him and so he killed it. Billy then entered to his first otter on the river Lyne accounting for it himself, near to where he had been bred by a joiner named Scott. The second otter he was entered to was bolted from a holt on the Lyne and hounds drove it off the river and into some woods, where it was lost, only to be found the very next day by a bloodhound belonging to a gamekeeper who worked for a Mister Standish.

'Sandy' eventually gave Billy to Doctor Grant who so impressed him when he hunted with Grant's pack of otterhounds, which was the Teviotdale Otterhounds kennelled at Hawick in Northumberland. I believe Sanderson's Billy played a huge part in the development of future strains of fell terrier. Billy was well muscled and had a massive head with punishing jaws; qualities which I believe he passed on to his descendants, which could be found all over Northern England. Fred Barker's Chowt-faced

Rock had a massive head and was well muscled and I believe he was descended from Billy, as Barker certainly hunted in the same districts as had 'Sandy' and so it seems reasonable to suggest that that country was amply populated with descendants of bull terrier, Billy..

I also believe the massive heads found on the early terriers of the Buck/Breay strain of fell terrier, later to become known as Patterdale terriers, were inherited through the bloodlines of Billy; via Bradley's Rip which was another terrier with a massive head. Sanderson was a legend in his own lifetime and Billy was one of his most famous terriers, so I am certain many bitches were taken to him and that his blood improved both bone and gameness in the resultant offspring. Though a bull terrier, Billy had a superb nose and he could both find and kill an otter, which made his breeding widely desirable to hunters of large quarry. I also believe these small bull terriers played a huge part in the breeding of fell, Border, Bedlington and Dandie Dinmont terriers.

Having mentioned Dandie Dimont terriers, it seems to be the right time to discuss some interesting facts about this breed, some of which I have unearthed from the British Library archives. Doctor Grant of Hawick, who hunted the Teviotdale Otterhounds, was also a keen terrier breeder and he kept Dandie Dinmont terriers and used them with his hounds. However, James Davidson of Hindlee, a yeoman farmer who lived in the wilds of the Northumberland hills, was the most famous breeder. Some writers claim that Davidson created the breed, but that simply isn't true, he was just credited in his own lifetime with having the best strains of pepper and mustard coloured terriers.

This type had been around for centuries before Davidson was born and what is more they were found all over Scotland and the Border regions. In fact, in those days they were very similar to some terriers found in the fells of Cumberland. Davidson was a keen hunter of foxes in particular, but in his day (he died in 1820) foxes were scarce due to much of the land being cared for by gamekeepers who kept predator numbers severely in check, so Davidson sometimes struggled to find quarry that his youngsters could be entered to. In such situations he decided that the next best thing to a tough hill fox was a cat, so he tried to "procure" one from a cottage some distance away from Hindlee (no doubt so that the owner didn't get wind of it).

His shepherd knew of his master's desire to obtain a cat and he happened to call at Andrew Telfer's cottage when he was out and about one day. A large female cat was dozing the day away at the cottage and on leaving, Davidson's shepherd somehow got hold of the cat and took it back to his master. Davidson had in mind a drain especially for the occasion, a drain which ran under a road and which was blocked at one end. Davidson put the cat in and then entered one of his young terriers, which went to the cat like wildfire, but which was beaten off within a few minutes, emerging with much of its skin almost torn off its nose and refusing to re-enter the lair.

Davidson was not particularly impressed, but he had a second youngster ready to try, which again went like wildfire. Again though, this youngster emerged with its tail between its legs, refusing to go to that fierce beast below ground. Furious, Davidson then put in his best bitch Tar, which was the ancestress of his strain, so this was obviously during the early days of his terrier breeding; sometime during the latter half of the eighteenth century. Tar was by this time a famous bitch and she had killed many foxes, but that cat put up such a valiant fight that even she retreated in the end. "Confoond the cat, she's tumblt an e'e oot o' the bitch!" exclaimed Davidson.

This made him even more furious and so he dug-out the poor cat, intending to kill it by throwing it to all three terriers, but she wriggled out of his grip and got onto a nearby stone wall, fleeing with the three terriers in hot pursuit. The cat eventually got into a plantation and disappeared. Though he searched high and low, Davidson could not find his quarry and so he was forced to give her best. Davidson's shepherd called again at Andrew Telfer's a day or so later and there, curled up enjoying her home comforts as though nothing had happened, was the large cat.

Ned Dunne of Whitelee at the head of Redesdale was another early breeder of what later became known as Dandie Dinmont terriers. His strain was of the old type bred by Davidson and they were described as being "long-bodied with strong, short legs and wirey-haired." It was also said that they were of a very quiet and shy temperament, but that they were fierce if roused and forced to make a fight of it. They worked well with hounds and other terriers and were run loose with both otterhounds and foxhounds.

The Rewards of Being Patient

John Finney always tried to hold back his terriers, even if they were begging for work. He learnt his lesson when he was a young lad, putting a Border-Lakeland terrier bitch to ground when she was just eight months of age. She encountered a badger and took a bit of a mauling for her troubles. From then on she was far too hard and lacking sense when at large quarry, so Finney chose to make certain he kept his youngsters out of earths until they were fourteen of fifteen months of age, though he allowed them to run unoccupied earths before this. He also didn't mind if his terriers wouldn't do much, if anything, during their first spell at large quarry.

He has known his terriers go to a fox, bark at it a few times and return, during a first encounter, but this has not worried him in any way. He simply tried the youngster again the next time and usually, nine times out of ten, the youngster would show much more interest on this occasion, very often staying until dug out, or the quarry decided to bolt. By the third stint to ground his young entry was usually finding unaided and either bolting or staying with their fox as long as necessary. Very few of his terriers needed more than two or three stints at large quarry before they at last caught on and settled to their work, though many of these had been used to flush foxes from dense undergrowth long before going to ground.

He tells a tale of one youngster which was working alongside its sire in dense gorse, after his small pack had shown great interest in the covert, which was difficult to penetrate in places. Fettler had sired Turk, out of his bitch Myrt, which was bred down from the terriers of Frank Buck and Cyril Breay, with a little addition of Lakeland blood.

Border-Lakeland types of the 1930s

Fettler was also bred out of similar stock, but he had much more Border about him than Lakeland and was incredibly sensible when at fox. Finney loosed Fettler and Turk into the dense gorse, but the fox had gone to ground. He was hoping the terriers would flush it for his pack to hunt, but they slipped into the earth instead. Turk had bolted a fox from an earth on the edge of some woodland in the low country – his first proper stint at large quarry, and he had been to ground on just one other occasion, but didn't particularly show much interest, but this time Finney could hear him hard at his fox when he finally located the earth, which was situated right in the centre of the dense gorse, or whin, bushes.

Fettler had also got in and so Finney knew his fox wasn't going to bolt. He located the pair quite quickly and marked the spot, but darkness was fast coming on and so he was forced to leave Fettler in overnight, as the young Turk emerged just as they were about to leave. He and one of the followers returned first thing the next morning and dug out fox and terrier. The fox was long dead and Fettler was trapped behind it. What delighted John was the fact that Fettler was trapped behind the back-end of the fox, which meant that Turk had throttled his foe before emerging. Turk never looked back after this and one of his best stints to ground was when he bolted a large dog fox out of a dug-out rabbit hole and then drew out the vixen. Turk was a big strong terrier, but Finney was quick to stress that he could get almost anywhere. He did some great work for the pack, as he was also superb at finding and flushing foxes from dense coverts.

John occasionally ratted with his terriers, if any farmer needed some shifting from their yards, but he never put a terrier to rat that he didn't feel was ready to go. Seven or eight months suited his terriers when entering to rat, though some were older, as the occasions he ratted were quite infrequent. Very often his terriers had already seen fox before being entered to rat. He agrees that rats can bite hard, but he has never known a Border-Lakeland be put off from working them. One of his bitches once worked several dozen at one session and she never even came close to 'jibbing' (refusing to kill a rat because of previous bites). He considers rats to be small-fry, though he does state that good ratters usually go on to make good fox dogs, in his experience.

Even when it was legal to do so, John Finney didn't take to badger digging, though he did engage in a few digs when he was a young lad. He much preferred to hunt and dig foxes and usually only dug badger by accident, after an earth had been marked and he had put a terrier to ground thinking a fox was home, or when a fox hid behind a badger in a fox earth, which happened on occasion. One four hour dig in a rockpile uncovered a badger and Finney was shocked to find 'Brock' skulking in a cleft between two large rocks, with the fox hiding somewhere beyond and out of reach. The earth stunk of fox throughout and he had never suspected a badger was in among the rocks until he had at last broken through. Fettler was doing the honours that day and he had held the badger all that time, though he had received a number of bites in the process. Finney simply allowed the badger to go unharmed and left the unreachable fox for another day. Regular bathing with salt water, a few stitches and a few days of rest soon saw Fettler right and ready to go again, but Finney much preferred to avoid such injuries if at all possible.

Entering Border-Lakeland terriers to quarry is a matter for personal decision, though in my experience the more experienced terrier enthusiasts tend to have more patience. Not only are they willing to wait until their terrier is mature enough for work, but they are willing to wait until it catches on and enters properly. There are no rules in this regard, as some take longer than others. Some seem to be made workers from day one, while others need several stints to ground before finally settling properly. Patience in this regard really is a virtue. Give a dog a chance. Give it time, if you will be working your young terrier. Never force things either. Gentle words of encouragement are enough. And remember to work terriers according to the laws of the country in which you live.

Finney tells a story of a terrier named Grip which well illustrates the importance of being patient and of allowing the terrier to develop at its own pace. Grip was put into a crag earth, in a cleft between the rocks, where the fox was skulking on a ledge a few feet inside. Grip went in and had a good sniff around, bayed a few times and then emerged, uninterested in further proceedings. The next time he was put to ground he went like a Trojan, charging at his fox and driving it to the end of the drain where Finney was able to pull it out, or, rather, where his hound, Merlin, pulled it out. So never write off a terrier which at first shows little interest in work.

One terrierman who worked his charges with a northern pack of hounds tells a tale of one of his Border-Lakeland terriers which wouldn't enter to fox no matter what he tried.

He was almost at the end of his tether when one day hounds roused a fox, which ran to ground in a crag earth after giving hounds a good hunt across the face of the wide sweeping moors. Risking much embarrassment, he decided to give his bitch one last try and surprisingly she entered the earth eagerly, disappearing into the dark recesses of the rocks, finding her fox, baying at it and then finally bolting it. She never looked back after that and the terrierman was glad that he had given his bitch time to settle to her work.

This experience also well illustrates the need to be patient with a young terrier, which needs time to mature in order to settle to its work properly. A terrier may not even look at an earth for months and then one day it disappears to ground and works like a Trojan. Some will go to ground and bolt foxes, but refuse to stay if they will not bolt. John Finney tells a tale of one of his bitches, Myrt, which was like this. One day though, she went to ground, bolted a large dog fox after a fierce tussle and then found and killed a vixen in the same earth. Finney had to dig her out and he told of his delight when his bitch finally entered properly.

Gryke was of a similar disposition. This was yet another of Finney's terriers which was bred out of much Border terrier stock, being descended from Buck/Breay/Akerigg breeding. He was a powerfully built terrier and Finney looked forward to entering him to quarry. He tried this dog at around fourteen months of age, to a fox in a drain that had been marked-in by hounds. Rush was baying eagerly at the fox, but it would not bolt. Finney thought it the ideal time to try Gryke, so he loosed the dog, expecting him to enter very well indeed, but, though Gryke went right up to the fox and had a little bark at it, he very quickly emerged.

Finney left him loose while Rush continued to attempt to bolt it, hoping the dog would enter, but he just went in and out of the earth a few times, until Finney decided to dig out Rush and her fox. The drain was around four or five feet deep and the dig was difficult, but Gryke never entered properly to that fox. The very next outing saw a fox marked to ground in a moorland earth, a dug-out rabbit hole on the edge of the moor, and Gryke was put in. This time he worked a little more seriously, but emerged about twenty minutes later. The fox wasn't going to bolt, so Finney decided to move off and draw for another, but Gryke, still loose, suddenly ran back to the earth, disappeared below ground and failed to emerge. John eventually dug-out his terrier, which had finished his fox, a big dog fox, inside the earth. Imagine if Finney had written off the terrier after his lack of interest during that first stint to earth and had got rid of him, as some do. A great terrier would have been lost, as Gryke went on to become one of the best terriers Finney has ever seen at work, and he has seen lots of terriers working to fox over the years.

6
SHOWS
[Pages 67-76]

Showing terriers can be enjoyable and classes for Border-Lakeland terriers are very often put on at working terrier shows and game fairs, with many hunts up and down the country also staging fundraising shows where terrier classes are included. 'Crossbred' classes are for Border-Lakeland types, though at some shows Patterdale terriers are also entered in crossbred classes. Classes for Patterdale terriers should be separate however. Border, Jack Russell, Lakeland, Patterdale and crossbred classes are put on at many shows and Border-Lakelands should always be entered into the crossbred class, not the Lakeland class, as some have been in the past.

Lakeland types, that is, those which are not Kennel Club registered pedigree terriers, have much sharper lines than Border-Lakelands and are judged differently, so make certain that you always enter your terrier in the proper class. At some shows fell type classes may be staged instead of crossbred classes and this too is where Border-Lakeland terriers should be entered for exhibition purposes.

The Correct Class

Crossbred classes are not exactly labelled properly, as many Border-Lakeland terriers are as carefully bred as Patterdale or Lakeland terriers and are a breed in their own right. In fact, they are an older breed than either the Patterdale or Lakeland terrier, as both of these have been created and developed from old fell, or Border-Lakeland type terriers, just as Border terriers were created and developed from the same rootstock, so crossbred classes are better labelled as fell type, or Border-Lakeland classes.

It is best not to take exhibiting too seriously, though it is also good to put in some effort to at least compete, giving your terrier a good shot at winning, or at least picking up a rosette. Shows really took off in the Lake District during the 1860s after the first dog show staged in 1859 in Newcastle started a craze which eventually had a massive impact on type. Those early shows were staged in conjunction with agricultural shows throughout the Lakes, though some became more prestigious than others and serious terrier breeding in order to improve type began to spread throughout the country, not just the region, during the latter half of the nineteenth century and well into the twentieth. Grasmere Sports, Rydal Hound Show (terrier section) and Keswick show, and those staged in and around Egremont, were some of the most prestigious and influential of the Lakeland terrier shows and any serious breeder wanted to win these events.

Improving Type

The old fell, or Border-Lakeland type, then known mostly as coloured working terriers, fell, or fellside terriers, was bred for work and so type was nothing special, with many terriers being of poor quality from an aesthetic point of view, so breeders set out to improve conformation and some smart terriers were already being produced as early as the late 1860s. Robinson of Egremont and Peter Long were two of the most successful early breeders of what later became known as the Lakeland terrier and Robinson actually made part of his living by breeding and selling typey terriers capable of winning at shows, despite some classes in those days having as many as a hundred or more entries in each class. Robinson and Peter Long had a massive influence on terrier breeding during the late 1800s and early 1900s, as did the Kitchen family of Ennerdale and Egremont.

Type varied greatly in those days, with some terriers displaying much Bedlington about them, while others, such as the old Patterdale type which, incidentally, was bred throughout the Lakes, not just in Patterdale, resembled workmanlike Border terriers, but with better coats. As early as the 1860s staff at the Melbreak Foxhounds bred and worked what were described by their Master, Squire John Benson, as "reddish, strong-haired and courageous" terriers and these may well have been early Patterdale terriers.

The old type 'twixt Border & Lakeland terriers

Willie Tyson of Ennerdale, Will Ritson of Wasdale Head and the Nelson family of Buttermere and Patterdale were some of the most influential breeders of the old Patterdale strain and Joe Bowman, Tommy Dobson and other Huntsmen used such terriers with their hounds. In fact, Braithwaite Wilson kept the old strains of Patterdale terrier, which he later undoubtedly infused with more typey Lakeland terriers after the 1912 meeting at Keswick Show had finally separated the old fell type from the new typey terrier which was becoming increasingly popular.

Braithwaite Wilson was great friends with Billy Ridley of Penrith, who bred the new type of Lakeland terrier and who often supplied Mrs Graham Spence with some of her best Lakeland terriers during the 1920s and 1930s. In fact, Ridley often gave her first choice on any adult dogs or puppies he had for sale, as he was a close friend of her kennelman, Mister Overs. A few of her champion Lakeland terriers were obtained from Ridley's strain, which produced a famous bitch line in particular, or were bred out of dogs or bitches she obtained from Ridley.

It is true that Braithwaite Wilson felt the new improved Lakeland terrier was threatening to ruin the old working terrier strains used with the famous fell packs, but I am certain he was referring to those breeders who were putting type above working ability and were breeding from stud dogs or bitches which hadn't been entered to large quarry such as foxes and otters. Wilson could not have been referring to the new improved Lakeland in general, as several worked with the Ullswater Foxhounds and they proved to be tremendous workers. The truth is that in really tight places Wilson would use Lakeland terriers bred by Mrs Spence and undoubtedly Billy Ridley too, as they were narrow enough to get almost anywhere and could bolt foxes from places where larger and bulkier types failed to get in.

Wilson also infused his old Patterdale strain, a strain undoubtedly influenced by the terriers of the Nelson family of Patterdale whose strain worked with the Ullswater Hounds for several decades, using the typey Lakeland stud dogs of the time, probably through both Billy Ridley and Mrs Spence of Howtown. As photographs indicate, Wilson's terriers were often too typey not to have been bred, at least in part, out of the new Lakeland stock.

While many breeders improved type on their old fell strains, some continued to keep the old type and throughout the decades since, many of these strains have survived down to modern times. True, several of these strains have been infused with Lakeland and, or, Border terrier blood, but that has done little harm to the old bloodlines, as Lakeland and Border terriers, as we have seen, are very closely related to the old fell, or Border-Lakeland strains, having been developed from them in the first place. Those which have been infused with Lakeland blood are very often more fiery and harder at their work than those infused with Border terrier blood, which often results in sane and sensible workers being produced; terriers which avoid bad injuries.

Lakeland terriers of the 1930s belonging to Mrs Graham Spence of Howtown

Patterdale terriers were partly bred from Border terriers too, the old original type kept by Frank Buck and Cyril Breay being a mixture of old fell bloodlines, Sealyham terrier bloodlines Breay brought with him to Mallerstang from South Wales, and Border terrier blood from the Bedale, Zetland and Lunesdale Hunts in particular. Josey Akerigg of Garsdale in the Yorkshire Dales infused his old strain with Border terrier blood and his stock was superb at work; so good, in fact, that Breay, Buck and a host of other terrier breeders, used the stud dogs of Akerigg to improve sense and working ability in their own stock. So modern Border-Lakeland terriers are best described as a mix of old fell terrier bloodlines infused with both Lakeland and Border terrier blood. Those which display much Border terrier about them are similar in type to the old Patterdale terrier in existence as early as the mid-1800s at Elterwater (this type was also known as the Elterwater terrier) which is situated near the Langdales.

Border-Lakeland terriers today, although not generally having the same class as the more refined Lakeland type, or the true breeding type of the Border terrier, are rightly considered a breed in their own right and some are very typey indeed. My own bitch Beck can be described as a Border-Lakeland terrier and she remains unbeaten in her 'crossbred' classes whenever I have exhibited. She is very smart when properly prepared for the show-ring, though I exhibit very infrequently these days.

Preparing for a Show

One of the keys to success when exhibiting terriers is to make the effort to prepare properly. Terrier shows where Border-Lakelands can be exhibited are not for the typical pampered pet which has been groomed until its hair is silky and soft, and adorned with pink ribbons, but still, some effort needs to be put in before a show.

I would not recommend bathing just before a show. A judge worth his salt will be concerned with, not only coat type, but he will also be looking for weatherproofing within that coat. A breed of working terrier should have an oily jacket as this will repel rainwater and thus protect the wearer from the elements. Bathing will reduce oiliness for some time after, so this is best avoided, or carried out a few days before a show. A good judge will rub the hair between fingers and thumb in order to ascertain the oiliness of a terrier's jacket. He (or she, of course!) will also be looking for tightness and denseness in a coat. This again helps repel rainwater and keeps cold winds at bay. A cold and sodden terrier would be at risk of dying of exposure when rainwater and icy winds get at the skin, so a decent jacket is vital. Border-Lakelands generally have rough coats and these can be greatly improved by stripping-out the jacket just before the show season begins, most of which are staged in spring, summer and early autumn.

A stripping knife can be purchased from any decent pet

store, or on Amazon or Ebay, or some other internet site, at reasonable cost and this is used to pull out the longer hairs which can look unsightly. Always remember to do this with the growth of hair, not against it, just as a carpenter works along with the grain, not against it. Pulling out the longer hairs will neaten and tighten the coat and will encourage new growth, hard and wiry new growth, which will appear within a very short time, when your terrier will at last be ready for exhibiting. Strip-out the long hair on the legs and paws too. Little stripping is usually needed around the head and face, though some stripping to tidy-up appearance will be necessary. Avoid using scissors as cutting the jacket will only ruin the wiry texture and spoil the colour.

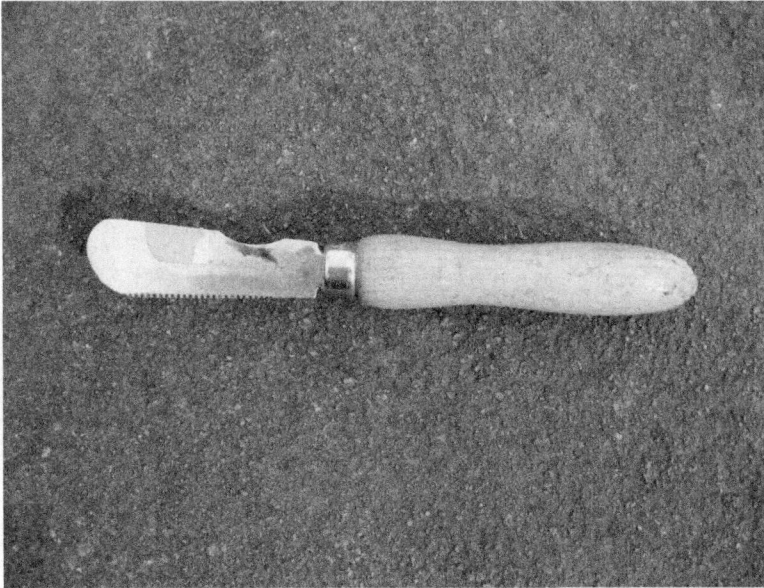

A stripping knife

Stripping-out the jacket is the main task of preparation, though it is also beneficial to make certain that the eyes are clean and that the terrier is neither too fat, nor too thin. A light grooming just before the show is beneficial, as is making certain that the dog generally is clean and of neat appearance. There is nothing more one can do, as judges will have individual tastes and will make up their own minds as to which of the exhibits will be given prizes, and in what order, though it is good to have an idea of what judges will be looking for in the show-ring. Do not forget, these are working terrier shows, so points which suit work will be considered when judging.

General Type & Spanning

The first thing a judge will look for is general type; a workmanlike appearance so as to ascertain that the terrier is not too big for the job or that it is not too long in the body, or indeed, too short in the body so as to hamper free movement. A terrier which is too long in the body will suffer back problems when working tight earths. One that is too short in the body may really struggle to negotiate tight and narrow places. So free movement and correct size, are essential qualities. Checking that a terrier is spannable is also vital at working terrier shows.

This is done by placing one's hands directly behind the shoulders of the terrier and enclosing them around the back and ribs. If thumbs meet at the top and fingers meet below the chest, then a terrier is spannable and can get into most earths. However, commonsense should prevail when spanning. If a judge has very small hands, for instance, then he could not expect his fingers to meet below the ribs. He must then judge the distance between and discern what is, and what is not, acceptable. If a judge has huge hands and a dog is only-just spannable, then it is likely too big in the chest. Each judge must use discernment when using such fallible methods.

Leg Length & General Size

Length of leg is less important than the spannability of a terrier required to work in what are often narrow earths. This is because a terrier can fold its legs under its body, or stretch them out behind. As long as a terrier is narrow enough in the chest to get below ground, then length of leg is far less of an issue. Again, discernment must be exercised when judging and experience will usually aid a judge in making correct decisions. A loose guide would be that a terrier above fifteen inches at the shoulder would struggle badly to get in most earths.

Dick Peel, Honorary Master and lifelong supporter of the Blencathra Foxhounds, tells tales of a famous terrier called Red Ike which worked with the 'Cathra during the 1930s (from 1933 to 1937 to be precise) and ran loose with hounds. Ike was a large terrier, at least fifteen inches in height, yet he could work out foxes from most places in the fells, such as deep borrans and the infamous peat earths found particularly in the Caldbeck Fells district. Ike, in fact, was a grand terrier to work, despite his large size, so a terrier should not be 'knocked' by a judge unless it is above fifteen inches at the shoulder.

Note the leggy terriers at Newlands with the Blencathra Foxhounds during the 1930s

Can a terrier be too small? Some very small terriers have worked with the fell packs, so it is difficult to say, but a terrier with very short legs would surely struggle to cover rough country and jump on and off ledges. A terrier with short legs will never match type in taller terriers anyway, so exhibiting such stock may be a fruitless pursuit. Again, discernment in making judgements is the general rule.

One thing I do like to see on a terrier are straight legs, though I will not 'knock' one with feet that turn-out slightly, as long as its movement is free and natural. Straight legs adorn foxes and they are incredibly agile. Straight legs have also aided terriers working narrow crag ledges in order to flush foxes 'binking' there.

Showing your terrier can be great fun, as can be entering them in terrier races. Some shows include racing, while many do not, but have a go, as this can be both entertaining and rewarding. My best result was with Ghyll when he was reserve champion in the terrier racing at Langdale many years ago. He was beaten to the championship by an incredibly fast and agile Jack Russell with very short legs, so think on before rejecting terriers with short legs!

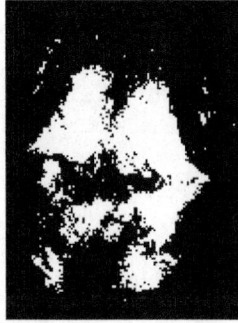

7
TERRIERS AT WORK
[Pages 77-91]

Terriers have been used in the Lake District for hundreds of years and by the late 1800s the little rough and ready tykes which later became known as fell terriers, and later still as Border-Lakeland terriers, had become famous for their abilities to work in the fells at a variety of quarry, often being run loose with hounds.

Most, if not all, of the fell packs hunted a variety of quarry until the early part of the twentieth century when the hunting of foxes alone became fashionable. This was also because other quarry such as polecats and pinemartens were very rare. Terriers before this time had been used with hounds to hunt polecats and pinemartens and had acquitted themselves very well indeed. In fact, a terrier was considered game in the fells if it would face a fast and hard-striking polecat or a pinemarten.

They were usually entered to such quarry before facing the fox, otter or badger in order to prepare them for tough times ahead. And such terriers knew what tough times were. They would have to cover upwards of twenty miles a day across rough country, before being asked to enter an earth, which could be incredibly deep and vast in area, find a fox, bolt it, or kill it below ground if it would not bolt (if a lamb or poultry killer, hard terriers were put in that would kill, not bolt, the fox). This was to put an end to lamb and poultry killing foxes and was a very important part of hunting in the fells. These terriers would also have to withstand very inclement weather which would easily kill off the constitutionally unsound.

Ernie Parker with terriers during the late 1930s or early 1940s

Finding Ability
A tough race of terrier was thus created and one that also

developed an exceptional nose for finding foxes. This quality was dictated by the landscape, as many earths in the fells particularly are huge, which meant that finding ability was an essential quality that was bred into the various strains. I believe German miners settling in the Lakes had a huge influence in the development of nose, via a long-backed small hound which they brought with them from their native land.

This hound was the ancestor of the modern Dachshund and, I believe, was brought to English shores by miners who settled in the north-east of England and in the Lakes too. These miners worked the Newlands and Borrowdale workings from the sixteenth century onwards and many lived at Keswick in rows of ancient cottages which no longer exist. Daniel Hechstetter, who imported these miners in large numbers because of the advanced expertise which wasn't available anywhere in Britain, even in Wales where later, during the nineteenth century, many Welsh miners would also come to the Lakes in order to teach the natives the most modern mining techniques, long after the Germans had returned home, though many of these settlers stayed and were "absorbed" into the local communities.

The exceptionally good nose of native terriers would have been greatly improved by the influence of these small German hounds which would also go to ground on fox and badger. Many of the early fell, or coloured working terriers were rather long in the back with large hound-type ears. The fact that many terrier packs existed in the Lakes before the First World War and the abilities of such packs to stick to a line like hounds does betray a hound ancestry, though all terriers were bred down from hunting hounds many centuries ago. This more recent hound influence would explain why many of these terriers have incredible finding ability when working often large earths typical of the Lakeland fells and other mountainous districts.

John Finney tells tales of his Border-Lakeland terriers finding foxes in very deep and dangerous old mines and of how they often bolted foxes from such places. His bitch

Rush, for instance, was exceptionally good at finding and bolting foxes from old mines found among the Pennine Chain, after other terriers had failed. Rush had an exceptional nose and could literally find anywhere. John also used her for working foxes out of seemingly impenetrable coverts and many times she found and flushed foxes from those vast places. She was so good at finding in undergrowth, in fact, that Finney was still using her on occasion when she was thirteen years of age; whenever a young terrier needed a little assistance.

Rush ended her career one winter's day when working dense gorse on a steep hillside below a thousand-foot fell. Rush found a fox, but it refused to leave covert and popped into a dug-out rabbit hole instead, where it turned to face the bitch. Rush, even at thirteen, had no reverse gears so to speak and so tackled Charlie head on. Her top jaw was broken in the encounter, but she survived and went on to enjoy a long and restful retirement.

Influential Early Breeders

Joseph Bowman was one of *the* most important figures in the early history of Border-Lakeland terriers, which were then commonly known as coloured working terriers. Bowman was born at Matterdale in 1850 and he was the eldest son of Matt and Mary Bowman who had married in 1847 after a short courtship. The couple went on to have another son and three daughters, but it was Joe who would become world famous in hunting circles during his own eventful lifetime, not only as an expert with hounds, but also as an expert with working terriers.

Matt Bowman was a miner probably at Patterdale or Glenridding where the lead mines gave employment to many local folk, but it seems Joe may have inherited his passion for hounds and terriers from his mother's side of the family. She was a Dawson and two of her brothers had hunted the Matterdale Foxhounds, which had ancient origins and which mainly survived by claiming bounties on the predators these hounds accounted for, which ranged from polecats to badgers, including foxes, wildcats and otters.

The Matterdale pack amalgamated with the Patterdale Foxhounds, a hunt owned by the Marshall family of Patterdale Hall, in 1873 and only a few years afterwards, in 1879, this pack began to be hunted by Joe Bowman, who had by that time grown into a very strong and healthy young man whose powers of endurance soon became legendary.

It seems reasonable to conclude that Joe's uncles took the young lad hunting, though as a miner no doubt Bowman senior also enjoyed going to meets whenever he got the chance and took along his young son with him. Young Joseph Bowman enjoyed a basic education and upon leaving school he began working in the farming industry at the Dalemain Estate with its distinctive pink stone house which lies close to Ullswater, 'twixt Pooley Bridge and Penrith.

Joe Bowman (blowing horn) & his Ullswater Hounds

After a spell of farming Joe left this industry to take up mining at the Greenside Lead Mines above Patterdale and Glenridding and there his arduous employment quickly transformed the weakly young lad into a strong and determined man, who, in the late summer of 1879, at just twenty-nine years of age, was offered the post of Huntsman at the Ullswater Foxhounds by J. W. Marshall of Patterdale Hall. This marked the beginning of a distinguished career for Bowman and soon the Ullswater became established as one of the more fashionable foot packs of the Lake District, with visitors travelling from all over the country to watch 'Auld Hunty,' as he became known, at work.

Joe first began looking after hounds when they were gathered-in during the early autumn of 1879 and they started hunting in October of that year, with the first official meet at Howtown in November, which charming little settlement is situated on the eastern side of Ullswater and which is the gateway to the wilds of Martindale, after Joe had walked his hounds from Patterdale to Howtown, going along the lake shore where the footpath can still be traversed to this day. The unofficial October hunting had seen hounds getting fit in readiness of the opening meet in November.

What a thrill it must have been for the young Joe Bowman to be Huntsman of the Ullswater Foxhounds after he had known what it was to live a life of real hardship whilst working in the mining industry. Not only was the workload backbreaking, but the miners faced constant dangers whilst underground. Poison gases were a constant threat, as was inundation from floodwaters, especially during times of heavy rainfall, not to mention the real possibility of rock falls.

The young lad must also have known that he ran a real risk of dying young if he remained in the mining industry for any length of time, as minute fragments of lead were often breathed-in when working in the confined spaces of the mines and these would settle on the lungs and slowly but surely suffocate the victims over time. Many lead miners died in middle-age from lungs that could no longer function to any effect after spending months, sometimes years, confined to their beds. Anthony Pool, the grandfather of that keen Ullswater follower Eddie Pool, died in this manner after a lifetime spent in the lead mines of Patterdale. Anthony Pool was a close friend of Joe Bowman and a keen terrier breeder who often used his charges with the pack.

One of many hunts that involved Anthony Pool was in 1890, on April 12th to be precise, which was discussed earlier, when he dug out a hunted fox using one of his many game terriers.

The young Bowman must have enjoyed a huge sense of freedom when he was successful in obtaining the post of Huntsman; a post which rarely comes available in the fells, and no doubt this fuelled his passion for hounds, terriers and hunting the fells of the Lake District. His sheer determination to keep with his hounds as best he could manage made him a legend in only a few short years and by 1890 his fame was growing rapidly.

During the early spring of 1890 Joe Bowman loosed his hounds on a lamb killing fox and a long hunt ensued, which resulted in the fox going to ground at Bason Crag Earth after hounds had severely pressed him. Harry Watson, the Whipper-in at the time, assisted Bowman and the pair were soon up with their hounds, which were eagerly marking in among the rockpiles.

Two of Bowman's best terriers at the time were Ullswater Whisk and Ullswater Tear 'Em and these were entered into Bason Crag Earth. The terriers soon found their skulking fox and bolted him, then turned their attention to another fox which was lying-up in the same earth.

Meanwhile hounds went away on the bolted fox, but the outcome wasn't reported. The hunt either fizzled-out soon after, or the fox was quickly accounted for, as Bowman and Watson then dug to the pair of terriers which were now hard at their second fox. It was a hard dig, as it always is in rock, but eventually they broke through to Whisk and Tear 'Em and the now very dead vixen. That was the end of the lambing troubles for that particular farmer.

On March 30th 1890 the Ullswater Foxhounds were at Selside for Bannisdale, where hounds took up a drag and, with noses to the ground, puzzled it out to Capple Fell where the owner of the drag was roused by Ringwood and Stormer. The pack then pressed him severely across the forest area and they turned him in by White How, with Bellman and

Wildfire now leading. They crossed Bannisdale Beck and hunted into the woodlands, the scent taking them to an earth in the woods, which hounds marked keenly.

Bowman and Harry Watson were soon with their pack and Ullswater Twist and Ullswater Tear 'Em were put to ground. The terriers quickly located their quarry and persuaded him to bolt soon after. A fast hunt then ensued and Wildfire, Layman and Towler eventually caught him. 'Jacky' was taken back to the inn and weighed and he proved to be a nineteen pounds dog fox, of a variety fell-hunters of old once called 'greyhound' foxes. This was the twenty-third adult fox accounted for that season by Bowman's pack, which doesn't seem a lot by more recent standards, but one must remember that in those days foxes were very scarce.

Up until the 1880s foxes, together with polecats, pinemartens, otters, badgers and wildcats, which clung onto existence in Martindale until finally becoming extinct in the Lake District by Bowman's time as Huntsman, had been hunted down by those who could claim bounties on their carcasses and so all such predators were scarce in those days. A lot of the areas were also heavily gamekeepered until the First World War and thus predators were not welcome on such land. A lot of keepers back then would put strychnine poison out for foxes and other predators, even up until the Second World War in those areas still keepered at that time, so finding and accounting for large numbers of foxes in those days was rare. Some seasons were better than others of course, but around thirty or so adult foxes accounted for in a season, prior to the First World War, was very respectable indeed. In fact, larger numbers of foxes were rarely taken by the fell packs until after the Second World War when fox numbers began to swell massively due to much less land being managed by gamekeepers, as well as a massively reduced number of keen hunting folk out on the fells and other Lakeland areas.

Before the First World War there was a tradition in Lakeland of hunting almost anything that moved with almost any type of dog that would hunt scent, or crawl into an earth, or rockpile. Packs were made up of terriers, hounds, farm collies and street curs and these packs were often hunted on Sundays by large numbers of farmers and village folk who got together regularly and often all year round in order to enjoy hunts with these 'bobbery' packs. Peter Long, the father of George Henry Long, was one such keen hunting man and he and many from the small town of Egremont would hunt anything from stoats to deer with a mixed pack if scenting conditions proved good enough.

Many of these keen hunting men, as well as those who had served as gamekeepers, didn't return after the slaughter of the First World War and so this tradition almost died out, being carried on by a few keen hunters even into the modern day, but on a far less grand scale. And so fox numbers have increased dramatically during more recent times. In Bowman's day foxes were found in very low numbers, but nevertheless the hunts were grand whenever scent was 'holding.' In fact, many of the hunts Bowman enjoyed were much longer in time and distance than most hunts of recent years, probably because foxes in those days travelled over a much wider territory due to low numbers.

There is an interesting account of a hunt involving Bowman's beloved Ullswater Foxhounds when they were invited to hunt the fells near Sedbergh, which hunt was discussed earlier. One interesting feature of this hunt is that the Ullswater Hounds had never before seen a badger, which tells us that they were incredibly rare, even non-existent, in those parts of the Lakes hunted by this pack at that time (1890).

Bowman likely inherited some of his terriers from those of Dan Pattinson who had hunted the Patterdale Hounds for a number of years and whose terrier stock was famous for being game. These early terriers were described in *The Field* by a correspondent who hunted with the Kendal Otterhounds in 1890 (possibly Rawdon Lee). This account appeared earlier, but I think it is worth repeating, as this description is fascinating and could be applied to some Border-Lakeland types of today. He stated that some of the terriers working otter in the Lakes were from a strain descended from the terriers of the Honourable H. M. Beresford.

They weighed around twenty pounds, were long and straight in the leg, long in the back, agile, with big ears (the influence of those German hounds perhaps!) and shaggy coats. Colours varied, but the most common were red, yellow (light tan), blue grizzle and black and tan. This description of the working terriers common in the Lakes towards the end of the nineteenth century, is fascinating, being more valuable because it was written by someone who actually kept, worked and bred the ancestors of modern Border-Lakeland terriers. Plummer stated that black and tan terriers were rare in the Lakes until perhaps the middle of the twentieth century (see *The Fell Terrier*), but my research suggests otherwise. Black and tan was not a rare colour at all, though blue and tan was far more common and was actually more highly favoured in those days.

Old Anthony Chapman, the father of George and grandfather of Anthony, both of the Coniston Foxhounds, was another influential breeder of the nineteenth century and early twentieth century, and his stock was very game. Chapman knew Dan Pattinson of the Patterdale Hounds and his stock may have been descended, at least in part, from Pattinson's terriers. On Friday February 8th 1867 hounds drew from Hartsop Hall after meeting there, which line took them over Kirkstone and to the head of the glorious Troutbeck Valley where Beatrix Potter spent so many years tending her beloved herdwick sheep, while sometimes enjoying watching hounds hunting in the area. Hounds dragged to Swine Crag and to Broad How Borran, where they marked-in. This earth is vast and very deep, having claimed the lives of a number of terriers over the centuries.

Pattinson had Banter, Crab and Jack by his side that morning and he put Jack into Broad How Borran. This was obviously a very good terrier, as Jack found and bolted his fox, which holed again at Tongue Earth, another notoriously difficult place. Reynard was bolted once more, but hounds forced it to ground again at Gate House Crag, where it was dug out by the Kentmere hunters and was killed by hounds and a terrier.

Willie Irving with the Melbreak Foxhounds & terriers in 1936

At the Eskdale and Ennerdale both Tommy Dobson and Willie Porter were serious breeders, though Willie Tyson, Will Ritson and later Thomas Rawlings contributed largely to the development of the early strains which gave rise to the modern breed. Josey Akerigg of the Lunesdale Foxhounds who resided at Garsdale in the Yorkshire Dales was another serious breeder of Border-Lakeland type terriers and the Border terriers worked by Joe Dobinson of the Zetland Hunt also played a major role in various breeding programmes. Dobinson's Border terriers also contributed greatly to the development of modern Patterdale terriers.

Another who contributed in no small way to the development of this breed was Willie Irving, the one-time popular Huntsman of the Melbreak Foxhounds. It is true that Willie bred mostly pedigree Lakeland terriers, but he also kept a strain of what he called 'crossbreds' which were actually true Border-Lakeland terriers, as he crossed his pedigree stock with Border terriers in order to produce sensible offspring which he used for bolting foxes and especially for badger digging.

I believe these crossbreds of Irving's also played a large part in the future breeding of Border-Lakeland terriers, just as his Kennel Club registered Lakeland terriers played a large part in the development of both registered and unregistered Lakeland's. His stock, for instance, produced Harry Hardisty's famous Turk, which is the ancestor of many modern strains, as well as a host of other noted terriers. His registered Lakeland terriers closed with foxes and killed them at the earliest opportunity, so he needed terriers with more 'stand back and bay' qualities when at badgers, or when he wanted a fox bolted. His crossbred stock proved very game and sensible and they were famed for their working qualities when Irving hunted the Melbreak Hounds.

Another who influenced early bloodlines was Mister Irving of Maryport who kept a pack of hounds and a few terriers for the hunting of otters in north-western areas of the Lakes and possibly to the outskirts of Carlisle. He kept a celebrated pack and his terrier, Rock, had become a legendary worker by 1863. Friday April 3rd 1863 witnessed the Maryport Otterhounds meeting at Broughton Bridge at seven o'clock in the morning. Hounds drew the River Derwent which was a river beloved to William Wordsworth, the famous

Lakeland poet, and after a long draw in fine conditions Careless, Swimmer and Stormer roused an otter and led the pack of ten away along the river in pursuit, though, because of the strong spring sunshine, scent was not of the best.

Harry Hardisty with Turk – a terrier with much Lakeland & Border terrier blood in its lines

After a long hunt, Ruby and Stormer marked a holt and Ruby managed to reach in and grab the otter, pulling it out of the holt, but it shook itself free and went away upstream. The otter went to ground again a little further along and Sailor eagerly marked the holt. Irving put in his terrier Randy, which was also gaining a good reputation as a worker by that time, but he proved a little too big for this earth and so the famous Rock was put in instead and he really got at his quarry. It was a very tight holt and so Rock had very little room for manoeuvre, so he sadly received a very bad mauling and was in a fearful state when he was eventually dug out.

 Mister Irving asked one of the followers to carry Rock home for treatment, while Stormer drew the otter out of the holt, the fight taking hounds into the water where the otter was worried. The carcass was later weighed and proved to be an eighteen pounds bitch otter. Ten hounds and two terriers had been on the river that day, but sadly Rock, a terrier which had done much good work at this hunt, died of his injuries and he had become such a celebrity and such a famous worker of the time that his death actually made the newspapers. It seems only reasonable to assume that Rock would have sired quite a few litters before his demise, as good working terriers were always popular for breeding purposes. A good working dog terrier often served many bitches and sired several litters. That also proved to be the last season for the Maryport Otterhounds, as they amalgamated with the Carlisle Otterhounds in 1864 to form the New Carlisle Otterhounds, which later became the Carlisle and District Otterhounds. John Peel used this type of terrier with his hounds, but his contribution to bloodlines is unknown.

 The breeders who contributed in no small way to the development of Border-Lakeland terriers are too numerous to mention in a book of this size, but breeders were found all over the Lake District, as well as in Durham, North Yorkshire and among the Pennine hills, especially in the South Pennine regions and in the Rossendale Valley area too, where the term Border-Lakeland seems to have originated, sometime during the later 1950s. This name became popular during the 1970s and 1980s, but is not as common a name for this breed of terrier at the moment. The name of fell terrier seems to be more popular these days, though, as stated earlier, Patterdale terriers are in vogue nowadays. Despite the competition from closely related breeds, the wonderful temperament and working abilities of Border-Lakeland terriers will, I am certain, ensure that they will be around for a very long time to come.

John Peel & his famous pack

8
TO BREED OR NOT TO BREED?
[Pages 92-102]

I have a policy of never breeding for monetary gain (though there is little money in terrier breeding anyway) and only breed a litter when I need a youngster or two to replace ageing terriers. I believe there are enough unwanted dogs on the planet and so do not wish to contribute in any way to this trend. I also believe there are a number of excellent breeders out there and sometimes I do not breed at all, but purchase stock from others instead. This, of course, is a personal decision and it is up to each owner of Border-Lakeland terriers to decide what they will do.

Some say that a bitch must have at least one litter during its lifetime in order to ensure good health throughout its lifetime, but I have found this to be untrue. A bitch will be fine if not mated, so do not feel pressured to breed if that is not what you wish to do. If you do decide to breed, then do so responsibly. I have had no serious health problems with any of my bitches which have not been used for breeding a litter.

If I wish to replace ageing or dead stock, then I do my utmost to find homes for as many puppies as possible *before* breeding a litter. This is not always possible I know, but even if you can find homes for one or two puppies besides those you will keep for yourself, it is at least something. Advertising in local papers or publications which deal specifically with this breed, such as the Countryman's Weekly, will no doubt succeed in finding homes for any surplus stock, but, of course, advertisements are best placed when the puppies are nearing eight weeks of age, which is the minimum age for a puppy to leave its dam.

The Brood Bitch & the Stud Dog

The main quality of both potential breeding terriers is a good temperament. I would not advise anyone to breed from a terrier, dog or bitch that is aggressive with other dogs and especially with children. Only terriers which are sound family dogs should be bred from. The ancestors of Border-Lakeland terriers were often kennelled with hounds and were worked alongside other terriers, so aggression was not tolerated and aggressive dogs and bitches were thus never bred from. This ensured mostly excellent temperaments, which makes this breed so appealing. Thus future breeders should aim to produce youngsters with equally good temperaments. Usually two terriers of good temperament will produce offspring with similar qualities.

Another priority should be to make certain that both the brood bitch and the stud dog are healthy and constitutionally sound, with neither having any serious faults. Good coat on both potential parents is also a priority, more especially if you will either be working or showing your terrier. A poor coat will not endear your terrier to any judge of a working terrier show. If your terrier will simply be a family pet, then coat may not be important to you, but it will likely be important to potential buyers. So good coat should be essential for both the dog and bitch terrier. Avoid using a terrier with a soft and silky open coat. The jacket on a Border-Lakeland should either be smooth (slape-coated in Lake District terminology), or rough and wiry, not soft and silky. A coat should not be sparse either, but dense enough to keep out the cold and wet.

Neither the dog nor the bitch should have poor mouths, either undershot or overshot. The teeth should meet in a strong scissor-bite. The ears should not be too large and they should be drop-ears, not pricked-up like those of a Scottish terrier. It is true that some Patterdale terriers have a prick-ear, which was inherited from Scottish terrier influence, but this is a fault which should not be encouraged.

Size is an issue, as this breed should not exceed fifteen inches at the shoulder, though around thirteen inches is a more desirable size. It is difficult to guarantee size in the offspring of a dog and bitch, but generally speaking if a dog and bitch are not too big, then most, if not all, of the offspring should not be too big.

Can a terrier be too small? If the legs are too short for the owner to cross rough country, then the answer has to be, yes. A Border-Lakeland must have enough leg length to cross rough hill country at a decent pace – at least that of a fast walking man or woman. If a terrier has to be picked up and carried across rough country, then it is too small. There is an interesting account dated January 1st 1852, when famous John Peel was still alive and his son, John, was running the family farm at Rusthwaite (William Wordsworth had died only two years before), which gives us an insight into the size of these early Border-Lakeland type terriers at that point in terrier breeding history. Mister E. Southwell of the Pheasant Inn, Maryport, held a rabbit coursing contest and it was stated that most of the crack terriers of the district were in attendance. Terriers were run in pairs at three rabbits, one after the other, with the one turning the rabbit the most, or catching it, being the winner (thankfully, this cruel "sport" became illegal in 1911 and seems to have died out completely by the time of the Second World War). In the fourteen inch class there were twelve entries and Mister Kennet's Nettle won, beating Mister Brown's Wasp. There were also twelve entries in the sixteen inch class (terriers were sometimes crossed with whippets in order to increase leg length and so larger terriers were common when rabbit coursing was popular) and Mister Tunstall's Tosh was victorious, beating Mister Martin's Venus. There was even an eighteen inch class, with eight entries. Mister Tunstall's Tosh was victorious yet again, beating Mister Ward's Pincher. Large crowds gathered at the event and Peter

Wilkinson judged, with Mister Blackburn and Mister Hemerson acting as stewards.

Turk – a leggy terrier, but spannable

Of course, those which worked fox in the fells would not have been above fifteen inches at the shoulder. Colour varies among this breed, but the main colours are red, tan, blue and tan, blue grizzle and black and tan. Some offspring are born black and this is because Border-Lakelands are generally closely related to modern Patterdale terriers. Many of the old fell strains produced black terriers and some still do today. Black terriers are best exhibited in the Patterdale, or black fell, classes. Sometimes a Jack Russell type is born in a litter and these are popular both as workers and show dogs. Until there are classes for White Lakelands (which seems unlikely), such terriers should be shown as Jack Russells.

The Stud Fee

Having found a suitable stud dog, one can expect to pay anything from fifty pounds to the price of a puppy as the fee, or the owner will ask for 'pick of the litter' as his fee instead, which is quite reasonable. Giving the owner of the stud dog first choice is usual practise, so it is best not to choose which you will be keeping until after the stud fee puppy has been chosen. If conception fails, then any breeder worth his salt will offer the free services of his stud dog when the bitch next comes in season.

Finding a stud dog is not always easy, but this can be done by scanning through advertisements and especially by attending terrier shows and getting familiar with some of the breeders who exhibit their charges.

The Mating

The bitch will come into season and the best time for the mating to occur is the twelfth, thirteenth and fourteenth days after bleeding began. Your bitch will be most fertile at this time. The bitch can be taken to the dog for servicing, though a successful mating will occur if the dog is taken to the bitch too. This is a matter for convenience and personal choice, but make certain, wherever the mating is to occur, that there are no other dogs or bitches anywhere near the breeding pair. Also, a small space is far better than a large one, as a stud dog and brood bitch can be worn out by running around a large enclosed area.

Create a relaxed atmosphere as best you can. Supervise the mating, but be quiet and relaxed about doing so, as dogs will pick up on nervous or excitable vibes. Other than that, leave them to it. They will usually manage quite alright by themselves, though sometimes a mating will fail to occur. My own dog Turk was put to a Bedlington bitch and she just wouldn't accept him, no matter what he tried. One can do nothing but shrug one's shoulders and accept it if a mating fails. You can assist by holding the bitch for the stud dog or even by trying to guide him in, should he be struggling, but even then some attempts to mate do fail.

High Lea Laddie – a grand sort (early 1930s)

A dog and bitch will tie, but the length of time a tie lasts for will vary. Sometimes they will tie for just a few minutes, at other times for twenty minutes or even longer. This time can be boring, so have a cup of tea, while keeping a close eye on the tied pair. A tie is vital for conception, so do not try to rush them. They will part naturally in their own time.

The dog will look abnormal when they do part, but the penis

will soon withdraw back into the sheath after a short duration and he will be back to himself in no time at all, though he will usually be a little more pleased with himself than he was before meeting his intended! Two matings are enough. This can be done on the same day if that is convenient, after the pair has rested for a few hours, though it is best to wait until the next day for the second mating. Make a note of the date of both matings, for nine weeks later a litter of puppies will likely be born, if all has gone well. This could be nine weeks after the first mating, or nine weeks after the second, depending on when conception occurred.

Care of the Pregnant Bitch

A bitch should not be mated until she is at least twelve months of age, but I would not advise breeding from a bitch until she is at least two years old, as by this time she will be both physically and mentally mature enough to cope with the demands made upon her. A bitch should also be wormed using a multi-wormer preferably from the vet before she comes in season. She should also have fleas removed from her skin and bedding. When worming and getting rid of fleas always follow the instructions provided.

She should be fed normally for the first four weeks of pregnancy and then one extra meal should be added. I usually feed cereal such as weetabix, with a little glucose and watered-down milk added, in a morning, with her usual meal given in the evening. This should suffice, though portions can be increased if necessary. Make certain that fresh water is always available and if giving extra drinks of milk it is best to water it down a little and take the chill out of it, serving it at room temperature or even a little warmer, not straight out of the fridge. Do not give too much milk, as this will likely be too rich and will upset her stomach. If you wish to use supplements, then talk to your vet and get the right advice before doing so.

In the seventh week get your bitch settled in her whelping box, which can be wooden, or made of sturdy cardboard. The bitch should have easy access, but you will want to keep the puppies confined once they begin walking and running around. Thus the sides of the box should be high enough to restrict the puppies, yet low enough to allow the bitch to get in and out easily. The sides must also be low enough to allow the bitch to see her pups, so that she doesn't jump on any of them when getting in.

The whelping box should be sturdy and have sides high enough to keep the puppies in, while allowing access for the dam

This box should be roomy enough for bitch and growing puppies and should be placed in a warm, but not hot, place; out of direct sunlight and far enough away from heaters to avoid discomfort to the occupants. The bedding can be shredded paper, which I find is the best material to use. This is easily disposed of and the whelping box is thus easily kept clean and infection free. Remember to inform your vet in good time of the date your bitch is due to whelp, considering that the second mating may have been the one which resulted in conception, just in case of any emergencies. Border-Lakeland terriers suffer few problems when whelping, but occasionally things can go wrong and an emergency call to the vet may be necessary. This is just a precaution and will likely not be necessary.

The Birth

Your bitch will become unsettled when labour sets in and will likely scratch around in her bed. Labour can last a good few hours, so be as relaxed as possible. Your bitch will sense anxieties and tension, so help her to be as settled as possible by keeping calm and relaxed (not easy, I know!). As the birth nears the pregnant bitch may vomit, but do not worry, this is quite normal. It is best to supervise the birth if at all possible, though you may wake up in the morning and all is well with the new family.

My bitch Mist gave me no choice in the matter, as she went into hysterics the night she was due, when I tried going to bed. I was forced to stay up with her and slept on the couch, as she screamed like a banshee when I attempted to leave her. She gave birth to six healthy puppies during the early hours and on the next night she again went into hysterics as I tried to go to bed, as though she was telling me not to leave her alone "with this lot!" That was her first litter and she took time to settle with them, but after that first night she was fine and proved to be an excellent mother. Keep a close eye on the bitch and if there are any complications it may be best to telephone for the vet. If the bitch fails to bite the cord, thus freeing the puppy from the afterbirth, then cut it yourself with a pair of sterilized blunt scissors, making the cut well away from the body.

The Growing Litter & Tail-Docking

After the birth is over, which may take a few hours, allow your bitch out into the garden, if she will leave her litter that is, while you clean out the whelping box. From then on clean it out regularly, for the paper will become badly soiled. Your bitch will take care of the puppies, while you take care of the bitch, giving her ample food and drink. At three days of age tail-docking can be carried out, but this is best done by a qualified vet, if laws in the country in which you live allow for this.

Worming can be carried out from about three weeks of age using products from the vet or pet store, but make certain you carefully follow the directions. Also watch out for the symptoms of milk fever, though this condition is rare. Restlessness, rapid breathing and convulsions, or fits, may signal this condition, so call out the vet immediately. This is a life threatening illness and must be treated as quickly as possible.

Stroke and handle the puppies as soon as the dam will allow this without being disturbed or upset in any way, and allow your children to carefully and gently handle them too, as this will greatly aid the socialising process. The eyes will begin opening at between two and three weeks of age and at around three weeks the pups will be beginning to take tentative steps around the whelping box. You will soon come to appreciate why those sides need to be high enough to keep pups in, but allow them out for play and exercise once they are steady on their feet.

Weaning

I usually wean puppies at around four weeks of age, though this can be done sooner if the bitch isn't giving them enough milk, or she is drying up. Softened cereal with warm milk is best for the first few days and then softened puppy food will suffice, such as a complete meal puppy food. By the eighth week they should not need the puppy food softened anymore, but should be able to tackle it dry, unless the instructions on the packet advise softening until a later age. Again, follow instructions carefully. Provide a drink of watered-down milk slightly warmed after each meal, but do not put a bowl of water in the whelping box with them, for obvious reasons. It will just be spilled all over the place, or will be badly soiled in no time. Never have deep bowls of water in a puppy's environment, or buckets of water for that matter, as they can fall in and drown. Like having children, think about their environment and of how you can make it as safe as possible. Exercise and play periods should also be closely supervised.

Continue to provide the bitch with extra food, but as the puppies eat more solid food provided for them after weaning, you can begin to cut down on that given to the mother. Use commonsense, if your bitch looks too thin, then feed her up. If she is becoming obese, then cut her food down. She will need less as the puppies reach eight weeks of age, when it is time to sell them on to their new owners. Do your utmost to make certain they go to good homes and one way to do this is not to sell them too cheaply. Ask a good price for them. At the time of writing a well bred Border-Lakeland puppy will fetch about £150.00, or even more if they are show winning parents. An idiot is less likely to pay good money for a puppy, so do not "give" them away by asking little money for your litter.

The only other advice I can give is to be diligent about keeping the whelping box clean. The bitch will clean after her puppies soil, but the bedding will still become dirty in a relatively short time, so clean it out regularly. It is best to exercise your puppies out in the garden if the weather allows and if the puppies cannot get out and the garden is safe for them, otherwise try to exercise them on kitchen flooring, which is easily cleaned, as they will create a mess very quickly. If exercising in the garden with a pond in it, then keep a very close eye on your puppies. Only a minute or so lapse in concentration could end in tragedy if a puppy falls into the water.

9

FIRST AID & CARE OF THE ELDERLY TERRIER
[Pages 103-106]

First aid in this chapter is about dealing with only minor cuts and injuries, not anything more serious that should be treated by a vet as soon as possible. This includes minor bites from quarry such as rats and foxes. Such creatures can occasionally be encountered by terriers kept as pets, not just as working dogs, so it is good to have in mind a few basics when it comes to first aid.

Treating Minor Injuries

First of all it is good to remember that cuts, bites and scratches need to be both cleaned and allowed to dry in fresh air, so it is best not to use creams which will only keep the wound moist. A moist wound is more prone to infection, so allowing the wound to dry up as soon as possible is essential to fast healing. In my experience, and I have treated many wounds over the thirty and more years I have now been keeping terriers, there is nothing better than a few dabs of TCP, or something similar, or just plain salt water, for treating minor wounds. Allow the treated area to dry naturally and do not cover with anything at all. Bathing such wounds regularly, maybe as many as four or five times a day, will keep wounds clean and fresh air will do the rest. Anything more serious than minor cuts, scratches and bites should be treated by a vet and bandages may be applied to some more serious injuries.

Checking the eyes after exercising and work periods is essential. Debris such as grass seeds can easily be removed or an eye wash can be applied in order to get rid of anything which may cause harm to the eyes. If you cannot remove such debris yourself, then a visit to the vet may be necessary. Such bits left in the eyes can cause infections, so they are best removed as quickly as possible. Regular grooming, preferably every day after exercise periods, will help drag out any thorns or other potentially harmful debris from the jacket and checking the paws is another good measure after exercise, especially after periods in the countryside. Thorns stuck in pads can cause major problems if they become deeply embedded, so do your utmost to remove these quickly. If you notice your terrier is lame in one of its feet as you are out walking then it is prudent to check the paws immediately, as thorns are easily picked up when they stick into the outer tissue of the pad.

Basic first aid and preventative measures such as those described may save you quite a bit of money which would otherwise be spent at the local veterinary surgery. Untreated cuts, bites and scratches and debris left in eyes, or thorns in pads, can cause infections, which then means having to visit the vet who will likely administer antibiotics, but it is far better to avoid such infections in the first place. It is not cheap visiting your local vet these days, so any way of saving money, as long as the welfare of your terrier is not compromised of course, is more than welcome.

The Elderly Terrier

It is sad to see a terrier slowing down as it reaches old age and one of the first things I have noticed in my ageing dogs is that they tend to get weaker in the back legs. A terrier with weakening back legs should no longer be worked to ground, as it will struggle to jump on and off ledges and agility in tight and narrow spaces may also have deteriorated, though no doubt it will continue to enjoy bushing work, or perhaps a spot of ratting.

The eyes may lighten, but this does not necessarily mean they are going blind. Some of my old terriers have had almost white eyes, yet have shown no signs of blindness. Deafness may gradually increase as a dog gets older, so stop working a terrier that is deaf and be careful at exercise when it is loose, as deaf dogs can easily wander and be lost. Micro-chipping will help recovery, but there is always the chance that a lost dog can wander onto a busy road and be killed, so take great care with the elderly and keep a close eye on them at exercise.

Be considerate & discerning
when exercising ageing terriers

Elderly terriers may begin to need less food, the older they get, so keep an eye on weight, cutting down food if you notice your terrier is becoming obese. Avoid obesity in older dogs especially, as this will only shorten their lifespan. A terrier fed correctly and exercised regularly will hardly ever be at the vet and it will go on to enjoy a long life, giving you much pleasure over a number of years.

Exercise of the Elderly
If you notice that your terrier is struggling with exercise

periods and is even reluctant to go out, then you may be walking too far. Shorten the exercise periods in this case and your ageing terrier will no doubt once again find pleasure in its walks. If your dog is persistent in being reluctant to go on walks, even though you have shortened them, then it is simply telling you that it has had enough. In such cases a wander around the garden a few times a day will undoubtedly suffice from then on, until the end of its life. The rewards one gets from a good-natured terrier are well worth the effort of diligent care and, as the terrier gets older, kind consideration.

10
LIST OF TERRIER NAMES
[Pages107-142]

Adder; A snake found in the British Isles. Its venom can be deadly to dogs, so care must be taken in places such as the Lake District and the Hampshire New Forest. One of the creators of the Patterdale terrier, Frank Buck, had a terrier with this name.

Archie
Adler
Aubrey
Aniseed
Adele
Avens
Alto
Arrow
Angelica
Aster
Alison
Alum
Allegro
Astie
Allie
Acky
Autumn
Auburn
Alder

Ash
Asher; the Huntsman of the Belstone Foxhounds in David
Rook's novel, *The Belstone Fox.*
Ashton
Alice
Addy
Abby
Atlas
Avril
Ava
Alf

Alfie
Alfred
Archer
Arnie
Arnold
Absynth
Barney
Bart; from *The Simpsons* fame.
Brunswick
Blenim
Becker
Beckett
Blethin
Blythe

Brett
Brian
Basil
Beech
Beechy
Baton
Breton
Burdoch
Bulrush
Bluebell
Broom
Bryony
Bugle
Beagler
Bugler
Buck
Briton
Baltimore
Bracket
Brigg
Blagg
Bragg
Bodie; James Herriot (real name Alf Wight) had a border terrier with this name.
Blackett; the name of the children in Arthur Ransome's *Swallows and Amazons*.
Blen; shortened form of Blencathra, a Lakeland mountain where Sharp Edge has claimed a number of lives over the years.
Ben
Benny
Betty; once a popular name for Lakeland terriers bred and owned by folk local to the Lake District in particular.
Barley
Boozer
Britt
Bruce
Briar; another English name for a blackberry bush.

Bow
Bess
Brow
Bowson
Blackberry
Bilberry
Blueberry
Berry
Borran; a naturally formed rockpile in the Lakes.
Bruin
Brunt
Brant; meaning 'steep' in old Lake District fell parlance and a term that is still used by some today.
Brittle
Bramble; yet another term for a blackberry bush.
Brock; an old country term for a badger, as in 'Bill Brock.'
Breeze
Bonnie
Bone
Biddie
Beano
Bantam
Banter
Basher
Bashful
Butcher

Badger
Bink

Bodger

Blacky

Blacksmith; a famous Patterdale terrier had this name.

Boss

Buster

Brick

Bricky

Bleak

Blue

Buzz

Bracken; my own dog is called Bracken and he is a real character and big personality.

Billy; another country term for a badger and a name frequently used for terriers in particular.

Bobby; I knew a Jack Russell terrier with this name. He was the leader of a pack running loose on a local farm near where I grew up and he was an eager ratter, shifting some big rats as they moved between food supplies and a warm bed in the barn.

Bedlam; a suitable name for a noisy dog.

Bella

Bingo

Blitz

Barker; an ancestor of the modern Patterdale terrier had this name.

Beck; a Lakeland stream, or brook.

Breck; from the hero of the novel *Kidnapped*, Alan Breck.

Buffer

Bitters

Brook; a northern name for a stream.

Barrister

Barrack

Betsy

Becky

Belcher; this name would have suited one of my own dogs, which belched very loudly after every meal. I must have laughed every day of the ten or more years I had him, before he had to be put to sleep due to the ravages of old age, but

only after leaving my wife and I with some great memories.
Brockley
Brinkley; the name of the dog featured in the classic film *You've Got Mail* – one of my all-time favourites.
Bellman
Bowman
Bruntley
Brandle
Baldrick; of *Black Adder* fame.
Bradley
Butch; another of our dogs. Butch was as tough as 'owd boots, having survived distemper when he was a puppy. This disease had a massive mortality rate during the 1970s, but Butch pulled through after a few weeks of seriously ill health. He died at the age of thirteen, after going to sleep under a bush and never waking up – a peaceful end to a hectic life.
Bertha; a hill not far from where I grew up is known as Big Bertha. It is a lovely wild spot and is glorious in August, when the heather is in full purple bloom.
Buster;
Bobbin; used for cotton. The bobbin-turning industry once flourished in and around the English Lake District.
Cherry
Charlie; an old English name for a fox, or one of the hero's of the wonderful *Darling Buds of May*.
Chance
Chancel
Cyril
Clement
County
Celery
Campion
Charlock
Chicory
Chervil
Clarry
Clover

Comfret
Comfrey
Cockle
Cockler
Corn
Cob
Cowslip
Cranberry

Chez
Chaz
Chancer
Cleeve; a regional name for a steep valley in Devon, such as those found on Dartmoor and Exmoor. This can also be rendered 'Cleave.'
Crag; a feature of mountainous landscape such as that found in Cumbria, Derbyshire and North Wales.
Crevice
Chain; as in the 'Pennine Chain.'
Cass
Cora
Cobbler

Cal

Carron; a place in County Clare, Ireland.

Cackle

Cackler

Carlton

Candle

Chandler

Channel

Clonmel; a Southern-Irish town.

Chorister

Choral

Chorus

Clegg

Cleggy; a main character in the classic *Last of the Summer Wine.*

Cassy

Candy

Candour

Canter

Caffrey; great Irish ale!

Crab; a popular name for terriers in the Lake District, particularly around Windermere, Grasmere and Coniston.

Clem

Clemmy

Clam

Clammy

Crofter; a Scottish farmer, or smallholder.

Croft; a Scottish farm or smallholding.

Champ

Caddy

Champer

Cliff

Cryer

Claife; as in Claife Heights on the edge of Windermere.

Chomper

Chomp

Corrie; a regional name for rockpiles under crags in the Scottish Highlands, where foxes, badgers and otters sometimes dwell.

Cairn; a natural rockpile in Scotland, known as a borran in Lakeland. A cairn is also what walkers pile up on the tops of mountains and hills, though the name originally applies to the naturally formed rockpiles of Scotland.

Crest; as in the crest of a hill.

Compo; another main character in *Last of the Summer Wine*.

Coin

Cleaver

Connie

Crete

Clancy

Cartmel; the village and fell in the south Lakeland area.

Cragsman

Craggy

Cashel; the Irish town and castle.

Crafty

Con

Carry

Carter

Cromwell

Crescent

Camden

Cass

Chad

Chatter

Chatty

Chess

Cheseden; a famous industrial valley in Lancashire popular with walkers.

Davy; one of the ancestors of the modern Patterdale terrier, which was a great show winner during the 1960s.

Dark

Debby

Den

Denny

Derby

Dibble

Dibbler
Dribbler
Drizzle
Daffodil
Daisy
Dandelion
Dewsbury
Dewberry
Dock
Dill
Dilly
Diamond
Darky
Dak
Dandy
Dusty
Duster
Derwent; after the river and water in the northern Lake District.
Dobbin
Dodd
Doddick
Doug
Daker
Deadlock; the famous hound in the novel, *Tarka the Otter*.
Dusk
Dusky
Dent; a charming North Yorkshire village huddled between the wild fells.
Daz
Dart
Dartmoor
Driver; yet another place-name in areas such as Dartmoor and Exmoor.
Dot
Dottie
Dobbie; another popular name for terriers in the Lake District. Tommy Dobson bred some of the ancestors of

modern Lakeland terriers and one of his favourites was called Dobbie.

Dick

Devon

Dell; a remote valley.

Dingle; yet another name for a remote valley, or narrow gorge.

Drayton

Dray

Dragman

Eric

Eskdale; A valley in the west Lakes, which is an area of outstanding beauty.

Ellie

Elsa; the lion in *Born Free*.

Exmoor

Eire; beautiful Ireland.

Etta

Elkie

Elkanah

Emma

Emily

Eyre; as in *Jane Eyre*.

Effie

Edge; the genius guitarist from U2.

Eddie

Ebby

Elsie

Etty

Elderberry

Elder

Elderflower

Elodia

Elymus

Erica

Ernie

Fennel

Flax

Flaxon
Fig
Figoro
Fleming
Farmer
Fury; another popular terrier name in the Lakes in particular.
Fern; another name for bracken.
Forester
Fisher
Fen; lowland landscape in places such as Norfolk.

Fly
Fell; Lakeland name for a mountain.
Fricker
Flicker
Fangs
Fipps
Fritter
Fran
Franny
Fox
Foxy
Ferodo

Floss

Frisk; taken from a Cumbrian hunting song.

Foiler; a popular name for fox terriers during the late nineteenth century.

Frolic

Fan

Fuss

Fanny

Fussy

Fleet

Fleetwith; a mountain in the heart of the Lakes, where Honister Quarry is situated.

Fog

Foggy; one of the main characters in the classic *Last of the Summer Wine*.

Fred

Freddy

Flick

Foss; a name for a waterfall and pool in North Yorkshire, where shepherds used to dip their flocks of sheep.

Fettler

Flock

Frock

Forest

Frederick

Foil

Fitz

Fry

Fryor

Freeze

Frith

Firkin

Flip

Flipper

Flapper

Flap

Flag

Flagon

Frankie
Gin
Garlic
Goose
Griff
Griffon
Gentian
Ginny
Grouse
Gromit; from *Wallace and Gromit*.
Grade
Grader
Ginger
Gem; a famous ancestor of the Patterdale terrier of today.
Grip; a popular name for terriers.
Griff
Growl
Growler
Gruff
Geoff
Gen
Granite; a very hard rock.
Glen; a valley.
Glenny
Gillert; legend has it that a dog of this name killed the last wolf in Britain.
Gypsy
Galley
Gallion
Gallery
Ghyll; a steep ravine in Lakeland.
Gill
Gillie; a river keeper in Scotland.
Gyp; a popular name for terriers in the Lakes up until about the 1940s, after which it fell out of fashion.
Gravel
Gordon
Gaffer

Gravy
Gradient
Gradely
Gad
Gadder
Gladsome
Glad
Gladys
Gercher; a London slang name.
Gotcha
Greta; a river that runs through Keswick in Cumbria.
Gator
Granville; a character in the classic *Open All Hours*.
Hatty
Hawthorn
Hollyhock
Hysopp
Horseradish
Hassle
Hassler
Hawk
Hawker
Heath
Hemlock
Honeysuckle
Hetty
Hooch
Hook
Heckler
Hobby
Hobbler
Hobble
Hunter
Huntsman
Henry; I once knew a boxer with this name and he was a huge, muscular dog. The family was never burgled while he was in the house!
Heather; as in a heather-moor.

Henchman
Hacksaw
Hacker
Hem

Honey
Hornet
Hazel
Hyacinth; as in Mrs Bucket from *Keeping Up Appearances*.
Hackle
Harriet
Hemmy
Harry
Helvellyn; a Lakeland mountain that has claimed many lives over the years, where the infamous Striding Edge is located.
Hedger
Hark
Harker; Tom Harker from the wonderfully evocative *The Shooting Party*.
Harmony

Harmonica
Hassle
Hassler
Hemp
Heckle
Ice
Iris
Iggy
Ivy
Icey
Ike; yet another Lake District terrier name.
Itsy
Imogen
Inca
Ickle
Inkling
Idyll
Isher
Ishla
Ismay
Islay
Jasper
Jill
Jitters
Jeeves; of *Jeeves and Wooster* fame.
Jilly
Jake
Jasper
Juddy
Jelly
Jakey
Jen
Jenny
Jet
Jed
Jude
Judy
Jess

Jessy
Joe
Jack
Jacky
Jummy
Jumbo; an old fashioned name once popular for early fell
and Lakeland terriers.
Jock
Jockey
Jim
Jimmy
Jig
Jaggers; the lawyer in Charles Dickens wonderful tale *Great
Expectations*.
Jud
Juddy
Jester
Jest
Jelly
Jel
Jemma
Jerky
Jerrod
Jarrod
Jarrock
Jonty
Jaunt
Jaunter
Kate
Katrine
Kim
Kit
Kitty
Kimmy
Kimbel
Kip
Kipps
Kipper

Kerry; a county in Ireland of outstanding natural beauty.
Keeper; the name of Emily Bronte's dog, which featured in Charlotte Bronte's novel *Shirley*.
Kelly
Kettle
Kettley
Kettler
Kendal; a Cumbrian town considered as the gateway to the Lakes.
Kemp
Karry
Kes; from the book and film.
Lucy
Lace
Lacey
Lavender
Lindon
Liquorice
Lyle
Lucius

Lucas
Lett
Letty
Lentle
Line
Lil
Lilly
Liner

Lyne
Lindy
Lad
Laddie
Loppy
Ling; another name for moorland heather.
Lintle
Liddle
Link
Lank
Lanky
Lumber; a great name for a mischievous puppy.
Lambert
Lumpton
Lana
Laura
Lara
Lister
Lawyer
Linker
Link
Lester
Monty
Mellow
Marigold
Marjoram
Mistletoe
Mustard
Malva
Marram
May
Meadow
Molina
Mercury
Mars
Mellick
Melling
Mantle

Mizzen

Mast

Massey

Morris

Mick

Mickey

Mess

Messy

Moss; a popular name for sheepdogs.

Myrt

Myrtle; popular in Cumbria for terriers.

Mischief

Meg

Megan

Mol

Molly

Moley

Malone

Mock

Mocky

Murphy; a good Irish name.

Mint

Minty

Minter

Mist; I had a terrier by this name and she was a real character. After giving birth to her new litter of puppies I got her all settled in and was off to bed, when she kicked-up the most tremendous fuss, as though telling me not to leave her alone "with this lot!" I had to sleep on the sofa and keep her company that night, though afterwards she was fine.

Misty

Miller

Mister

Muster

Maple

Maggie

Mags

Miner; a good name for a terrier, which were originally bred

to go down holes in the ground.
Mona
Mel
Melly
Melbreak; a fell above Crummock Water in the Lakes.
Magda
Midge
Midget
Mac
Mike
Major
Marshal
Milly
Marsh
Mallow
Mickle
Mickeline
Mite
Matey
Mangle
Nancy
Nip
Nipper
Nippy
Nightingale
Nightshade
Nickel
Nidge
Nigel
Nell
Nellie
Newsboy
Narvik
Ness
Nessy; affectionate nickname for the mysterious Loch Ness
Monster.
Nessa
Nettle

Nelson
Nectar
Nicely
Nan
Nance
Nanny
Narnia
Nando

Ossler
Oscar
Onion
Oregamo
Ottis
Oat
Orchid
Orchard
Orca; of killer whale fame.
Otter
Oxen
Ox
Oz; from the famous film.
Ozzy
Oak
Oaken
Oakley
Otto
Ode
Oddjob

Ockle
Okra
Polly
Pinky
Primrose
Perk
Perks; a character out of the wonderful tale *The Railway Children.*
Polar
Perky
Printer
Parsley
Parsnip
Pansy
Pearl
Peppermint
Peter
Pike; a name associated with Lakeland mountains, as well as a fish popular with anglers.
Piker
Pennine; a mountain chain in England running from Derbyshire into the borders of England and Scotland, and very popular with walkers.
Pen
Penny
Prunella
Pilot
Paddy
Perry
Pestle
Purple
Pat
Patty
Poker
Pobble
Pedal
Pedlar
Peeler; another name for a policeman in Ireland.

Preston
Piper; a common name for terriers in the north-east of England.
Percy
Pep
Pepper
Pauper
Pamper
Phoenix
Pitcher
Peppy
Pip; the hero of the novel *Great Expectations*.
Pet
Petty
Port
Porter
Punch
Pickle
Patch
Prickle
Pig
Piggy
Pont
Panda
Promise
Porthole
Quill
Quiller
Queen
Queenie
Quantum
Quartz
Quell
Queller
Quarry
Quarryman
Roger
Rice

Raspberry
Rhubarb
Rose
Rosey
Rosemary
Ralph
Rattle
Rye
Rudyard
Rush
Royal
Renegade
Renny
Rennard
Renold
Rigg; place-name and a name for fells in the Lakes.
Ranter
Ransom
Russland
Russ
Rags
Race
Racer
Riff
Ruff
Ruffler
Rift
Riss
Rick
Ricky
Rock
Rocky
Red
Reel
Reeler
Rebel
Rex
Rydal; a small place in Cumbria between Ambleside and

Grasmere.
Rusty
Rattler
Ruthless
Ruth
Roy
Rastus
Rufford; a place near Sherwood Forest.
Robin
Ross
Rally
Ridge
Reef
Reeder
Reed
Ranger
Romper; a good name for the lively sort!
Runswick
Randy; a terrier which worked with the Maryport Otterhounds.
Steel
Spout
Steeler
Schooner
Swallow; the boat of *Swallows and Amazons*.
Spout
Spark
Sparky
Skiffle
Sid
Sidney
Selwyn
Stan
Stanley
Snap
Snapper
Snappy
Snatch

Sally
Sal
Scandal
Spiff
Spiffy
Stream
Snip
Sett
Settle
Settler
Sherry
Scamp
Shandy
Socks
Sam
Sammy
Samuel
Storm
Stormer
Smithy; shortened title for a blacksmith.
Smitty
Squeak
Squeaky
Squeaker
Stump
Stumpy
Sheena
Spider
Sassy
Silver
Silk
Silky
Selkie
Skip
Skipper
Skippy; of *Skippy the Kangaroo* fame.
Sedge
Smudge

Smudger
Sting
Stinger
Sharp
Sharper
Sharpy
Sharky
Scree; loose rock found on the fellsides in the Lake District.
Slate
Selwyn
Spiffy
Shandy
Sheena
Saffron
Sage
Shallot
Sorrel
Shepherd
Strawberry
Samphire
Star
Snowdrop
Silas
Slater
Slatt
Shake
Shaker
Skaky
Slattery
Sheik
Shallow
Sherman
Sheila
Shiraz
Scrag
Tar
Tim
Tarragon

Thistle
Thyme
Traveller
Tway
Tay
Tween
Timothy
Thwaite
Trim
Trimmer
Timmy
Tess
Tessy
Tessa
Tessle
Tressle
Tipple
Tippler
Tuppence
Trent; a river that flows through Nottinghamshire.
Trencher
Trench
Tweel
Twyne
Tweed; a famous salmon fishing river in Scotland.
Tweedy
Titch
Titchy
Techy
Tickle
Tickler
Tarn; a small body of water usually found out on the fells of the Lake District.
Tat
Tats
Tatters
Tatty
Teddy

Ted
Trace
Tracer
Topple
Toppler
Tink
Tinker
Tinky
Tyson
Tan
Tanner
Tandy
Tear 'Em; a famous name for terriers in the fells of Cumbria.
Twist
Twister
Tiger
Tigress
Tigger
Tiggle
Tig
Tarzan
Trouble
Teeze
Teezer
Teezy
Tizzy
Tip
Tippler
Trader
Tex
Texas
Texan
Taffy
Tangy
Tango
Taff
Trilby
Terry

Turban
Topsy
Topol
Toppy
Toppler
Turk; an old Scottish farming term and a Scottish place-name, as in Brig O' Turk.

Tarquin
Tarka; as in *Tarka the Otter*, a famous novel and film.
Tom
Thomas
Tommy
Tomlin
Trix
Trixie
Tina
Tony
Tangy
Tartar
Tyrant
Trick
Tricky
Trickster
Trap
Trappy
Trinket
Tack
Twile

Thorn
Thornton
Thornham
Thornly
Task
Tasker
Tasky
Tyne; a famous north-east river.
Tynedale
Tab
Tabby
Ulpha; a place in Lakeland.
Ulster
Ultra
Uz
Uzzar
Uckle
Uist
Vandal
Venus
Vim
Vimmy
Vixen
Venture
Viper; another name for an adder.
Vicky
Vic
Venom
Vent
Vee
Vye
Vermont
Vender
Vimto
Vintner
Vinnie
Violet
Vernon

Veronica
Vetch
Viola
Whip
Wallace; of *Wallace and Gromit* fame.
Whippy
Whin
Whinny
Wren
Woodruff
Woody; as in *Woody Woodpecker*.
Woodman
Warren
Wilmot
William
Worry
Willow
Winnow
Wist
Wisty
Wister
Welcome
Wasp; another common name for fell and Lakeland terriers.
Wendy
Whisky
Whisk
Whiskers
Will
Whitby
Witty
Whittle
Whittler
Willie
Wanton
Worton
Xanadu
Xavier
Xeres

York
Yorkshire
Yoeman; a gentleman farmer.
Yarrow; a yellow wild flower.
Yetty
Yellow
Yell
Yak
Yaz
Yasmin
Yum
Yummy
Zena
Zealot
Zebra
Zidan
Zeb
Zebby
Zak
Zad
Zadie
Zakry
Zinca
Zinky
Zinc
Zondra

Other books by Sean Frain:
The Lakeland Terrier
The Patterdale Terrier
Cumbrian True Crimes – Murder & Mystery in the Lakes
The Lake District – A Visitor's Miscellany
The Year of the Working Terrier

Border-Lakeland terriers have great temperaments and are full of character – they are a delight to own